Department of the Environment

Tower of London
The White Tower

Stories and
Models of
Famous Places

H T Sutton and P T Hammond

Her Majesty's Stationery Office

First published 1977

ISBN 0 11 670339 3

Contents

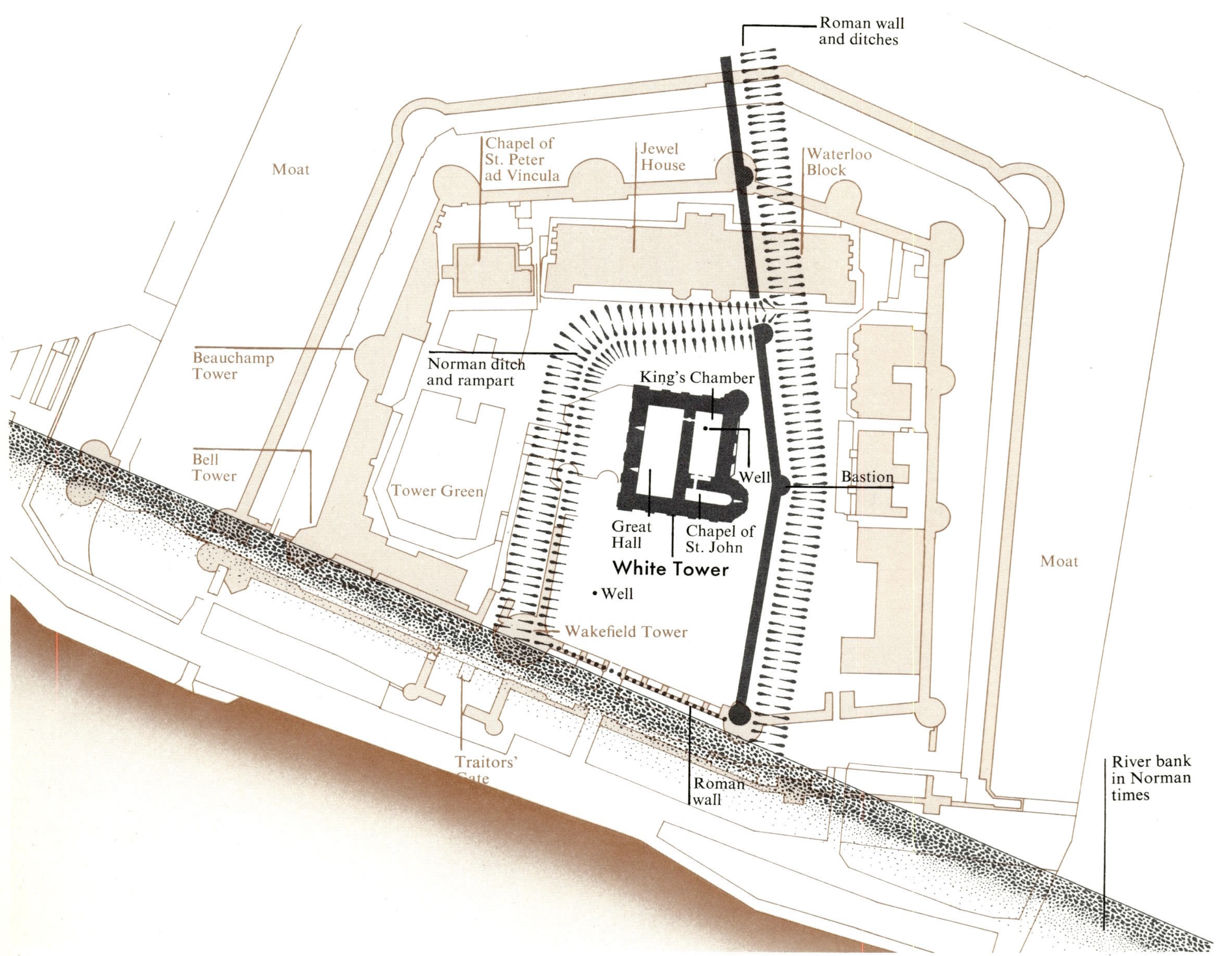
Roman wall and ditches
Moat
Chapel of St. Peter ad Vincula
Jewel House
Waterloo Block
Beauchamp Tower
Norman ditch and rampart
King's Chamber
Well
Bastion
Bell Tower
Tower Green
Great Hall
Chapel of St. John
White Tower
Moat
• Well
Wakefield Tower
Traitors'
Roman wall
River bank in Norman times

Preface

The Tower of London is more than nine hundred years old. At first it was quite small, only an earth mound with a wooden tower on top and a ditch all round. Then a great stone tower was built – the White Tower – which is still the keep of London's famous castle beside the River Thames. It is believed that, for a short time, the White Tower and the little wooden tower stood together inside the castle walls. Then the wooden tower was pulled down and the mound was levelled so that the White Tower stood alone. It became a place of refuge for kings and queens in time of rebellion and a palace for them in peacetime. It was a prison for some unhappy people and a home for others more fortunate. It has seen exciting days.

This book is about the earliest days when the Tower of London was very young. There are stories about people who helped to build the Tower or who once lived in it. There are ideas for things to do and to see when you visit the Tower. And you yourself can be one of the builders if you make the models which are part of each chapter in the book. It really does not matter whether you visit the Tower before or after you have made the models. If you come before, you will have seen the Tower for yourself and then be able to add your own ideas to the models. If you come afterwards you can compare your models with the real thing. But if you can manage it, the best way of all is to make two visits, once before you have started this book and again after you have made the models, read the stories and know about the things to do and see at the famous Tower of London.

1 The Wooden Tower

'Can I go out now, Mother?' asked Edmund.

'Your father says it is not yet safe,' his mother replied. 'There are Norman soldiers in the streets. People say they are still burning and looting in the villages round London.'

'I shall be very careful,' promised Edmund.

'Wait until your father comes home,' she said.

It was the year 1066 and Edmund's parents lived in London, near the Church of All Hallows. William of Normandy had invaded England and Harold, England's king, had been killed in a battle near Hastings. There had been fighting round London, and although the old city walls had kept the Normans out, Southwark on the other side of the Thames had been burned to the ground.

People were saying that England would soon be ruled by foreigners, and London was strangely quiet as everybody awaited the outcome of events.

'Oh dear,' sighed Edmund. 'I do wish I could go out!'

At this moment, Edmund's father returned home. He looked tired and sad. 'It is all over,' he said. 'William has been asked to become our king and he has agreed. We are all to be slaves of the Normans. It is a bad day for England!'

'But is there peace?' asked Edmund's mother.

'Aye. There is peace,' replied her husband. 'But I would fight on rather than be a servant to some Norman lord!'

As his parents talked, Edmund slipped quietly out of the house and made his way up the narrow street to find his friend Alfred. The news of peace had spread quickly and there were people at every corner, discussing the situation.

Alfred was pleased to see him. 'Let us go to the wall,' he suggested. 'We can see if the fighting has ended.'

The place to which the boys now made their way was a very special corner where they liked to play. The tall city wall reached the river at this point, and just where it turned to

run along the river bank the boys would play chain-he, hide and seek and other favourite games among the piles of old masonry which littered the ground. Edmund's father had told him that those old stones and bricks, and the city walls, had been left by people called 'Romans'. Like the Normans, they also were invaders who conquered England and they had built city walls to protect London from enemies.

As the wall came into sight, Edmund raced ahead to be there first. But then he stopped very suddenly. 'Look there!' he said, and he sounded very scared.

There were Norman soldiers standing in a group just where the boys liked to play!

'Let's go,' whispered Edmund.

But at this moment one of the soldiers saw the boys and beckoned to them. 'Come here,' he called. And his words were not easy to understand for he had a strong foreign accent. 'Do not be afraid,' he said, 'we wish to ask you a question.'

'Shall we?' whispered Edmund.

His friend nodded. And the two boys walked slowly across to the soldiers. As they approached, the other soldiers laughed and Edmund heard them speak to one another in a foreign language. It was, of course, the French language which was spoken in Normandy.

'My friends say that we should search you for weapons,' the English-speaking soldier told them, with a smile. 'They are joking.' Then he looked more serious. 'You Saxons are good fighters and we have to be careful. That is why we are going to build a castle here. To keep you Londoners in order!'

Edmund and Alfred looked puzzled. 'What is a castle, sir?' asked Edmund.

'It is a strong place which can be defended against an enemy,' explained the soldier. 'When King William comes to London we shall have the castle ready so that if you Londoners are stupid enough to attack him, he can use the castle to fight you off!' He pointed round the walls – just where the boys liked to play. 'All this,' he told them, 'will be part of our castle.'

Edmund began to see what his father meant when he said that peace was not worthwhile if all Saxons were to be slaves of Normandy. He looked angrily at the soldiers. 'What do you want us for, sir?' he asked.

'We shall need water in our castle,' the soldier told him. 'Where is the nearest well?'

'There is one . . .' began Alfred.

But Edmund interrupted him. 'The nearest one is just over here,' he said, and he led the soldier to a hole in the ground a few metres along the wall. The soldier looked down into the deep hole. He threw a stone in and in the depths he heard a splash.

'Good boy,' he told Edmund. 'Go home now, you are not allowed here. It is a forbidden place for all Saxons.'

'Why did you tell the soldier that was a well?' asked Alfred, as the boys walked home. They had both drawn water from it and found it black and smelly.

Edmund laughed. 'Because they are our enemies,' he said. 'Perhaps they will all drink from it and die of poisoning!'

For many days afterwards the boys went to watch the castle being built although they were careful not to be seen by the soldiers they had tricked.

The Normans had rounded up several hundred young men and put them to work digging a deep ditch along the two sides which were not protected by the city walls. In the corner, just where the boys used to play, some very tall and thick poles towered above the walls. Earth from the ditch was being packed in around the base of these poles to hold them upright. More and more earth was piled round the poles until

a third part of them was buried and a tall mound began to grow round them. The boys soon saw what the tall poles were for. They formed the framework for a wooden tower which the Normans built on top of the mound. This was London's first castle.

'But it is made of wood!' exclaimed Edmund, when he saw what they were doing. 'That will not be very difficult to knock down!'

'It's not nearly as big as the Abbey of Westminster,' said his friend. 'These Normans are not much good at building, are they?'

But as the work on the castle continued, they began to see how it would not be easy to attack. The tower was protected by a tall fence which ran right round the top of the high mound. The sides of the mound sloped steeply into the deep ditch which the men had dug.

There was a small entrance with strong wooden doors. With the high city walls on two sides and the ditch and fence on the other two sides, the castle was well protected all round. Within the wall and below the mound there were dwelling huts and other buildings for the soldiers who were to defend the castle.

One day, when the castle was almost finished, there was news that William of Normandy was coming to London to be crowned king in Westminster Abbey.

Edmund's father and many of his fellow Londoners said that they would never have a Norman as their king.

'Why, he cannot even speak English!' they told each other.

They were so angry that Edmund expected to see them take up arms again to turn the Normans out of London and prevent William being crowned. But as the days passed, more and more Norman soldiers arrived at the Tower of London and the people soon saw that it would be hopeless to rebel.

On Christmas Day, 1066, William of Normandy went to Westminster Abbey and was made King William the First of England.

The little wooden Tower of London had done its duty.

Things to look at and to do 1

1. Close to the White Tower you will find part of the Roman wall and the base of a Roman bastion or wall-tower. There is another section of the wall to be seen near Tower Hill Underground Station, in Wakefield Gardens. Notice how the walls were built. The Romans used a different kind of mortar from the Normans. They also built courses of tile-like bricks into their stone walls to strengthen them.

2. Roman pottery and tiles have been found near the White Tower. You can see them in the Beauchamp Tower. Look out for the tile with the print of a dog's paw in it.

3. The Normans built other castles as well as the Tower inside strong walls left by the Romans. Two of these were at Pevensey and Portchester. At each the Normans made one corner of the Roman fort into the yard or bailey of their castle, using the Roman walls on two sides and building a wooden fence on the other sides.

4. At the Tower, the Normans dug a ditch to make the bailey where the Roman wall stopped. Later the ditch was filled in, but now the soil has been removed from that part of the ditch north of the Wakefield Tower. You will also see the wall which was built in the middle of the ditch about two hundred years later.

Section of the Roman wall near the White Tower

5. Inside the bailey of Norman castles there was often a mound or motte, on which a wooden tower was built, like the tower in the first story. There is no trace of a motte at the Tower of London, but there are many motte and bailey castles you can still see, like the one in the picture which is at Berkhamsted. Perhaps there is a motte and bailey castle near your home which you can visit?

6. As the story says, every castle needed a

Portchester Castle

Berkhamsted Castle

well so that the soldiers could be sure of a water supply. At first there were probably two wells at the Tower. One can still be seen in the basement of the White Tower. The Normans dug it and lined it with stone while they were building the White Tower. See it and guess how deep it is. The other well was inside the bailey of the first castle, about fifteen metres south of the southwest corner of the White Tower. Now it is covered over and cannot be seen. This was probably the first well the Normans dug.

7. William claimed that the Saxon king, Edward the Confessor, who was made a saint after his death, had said that when he died William should rule England, and that Harold (who was later killed at Hastings) had no right to be king. In the Jewel House you will see

St Edward's Crown

St Edward's Crown. It was actually made for Charles II in 1661, but pieces of the real St Edward's Crown were worked into it.

8. You will see All Hallows Church on your way into the Tower. It was badly bombed in the Second World War and had to be rebuilt. Inside there are remains not only of the Saxon church but also bricks and a pavement which were part of a Roman building which was there before the church was built.

9. The Bayeux Tapestry tells the story of William's invasion of England in a series of pictures like a strip cartoon. Here some Saxon labourers are helping the Normans to build a castle at Hastings. The story of the building of the first Tower of London would make a good tapestry or strip cartoon. You might like to design one.

Model 1: The Wooden Castle

The photographs which follow show how to make a model of the wooden tower on its little hill. If you follow the instructions you will have a complete model of the castle inside the bailey where the White Tower was later built. If you want to make *only* the wooden tower, start work at picture number 19 and finish at number 27.

Part 1
The bailey and outer walls

You will need:

16 detergent packets
a large sheet of polythene
old newspapers
modelling clay (Newclay)
corrugated paper
yellow and blue powder paints
cocktail sticks or matchsticks
Plasticine (2 packets)
2 strawboards or a thick card 120cm × 85cm

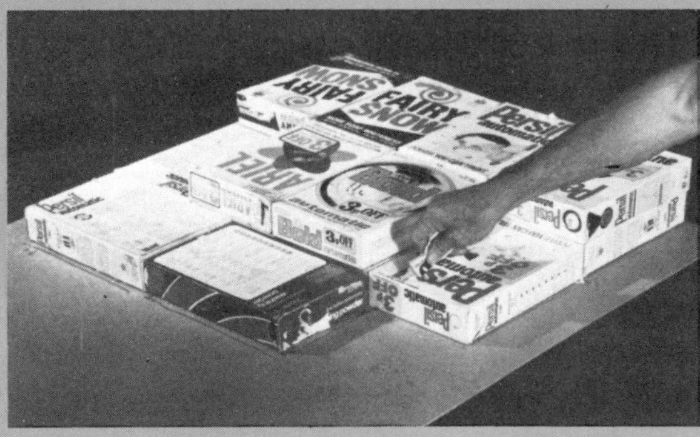

1. Take 2 strawboards or a sheet of thick card about 120 cm × 85 cm. Build a hillside of packets (16 detergent packets are shown in the picture). Glue the packets to each other and to the base.

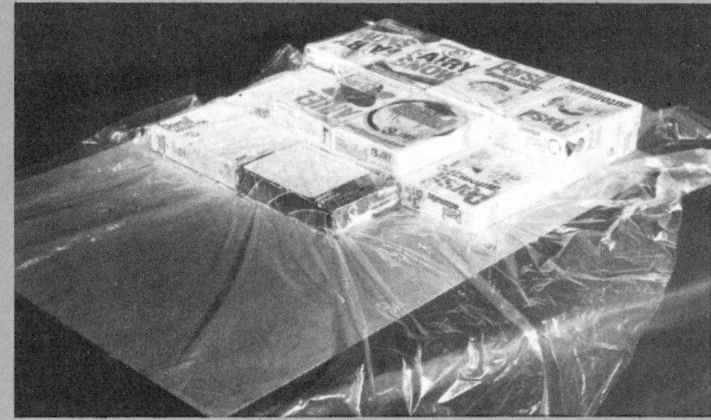

2. Cover the card and hillside with a large sheet of polythene. Do not glue it into position.

3. Soak several newspapers in water with a little washing-up liquid added. Soak for about 5 minutes. Squeeze the water out of a newspaper and then . . .

4. . . . open it out flat and lay it on the hillside . . .

5. . . . until it is completely covered. Rolled-up newspapers make the walls round the outside. The Roman wall part should have flattened top and sides; the rampart section should be rounded.

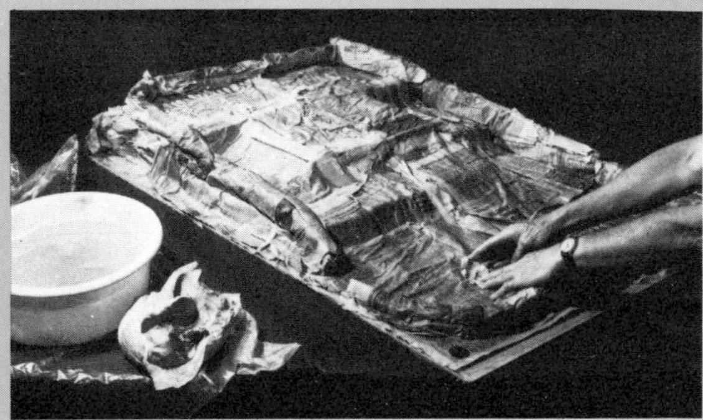

6. Take some Newclay. Soften it in water and spread it thinly over the wet paper . . .

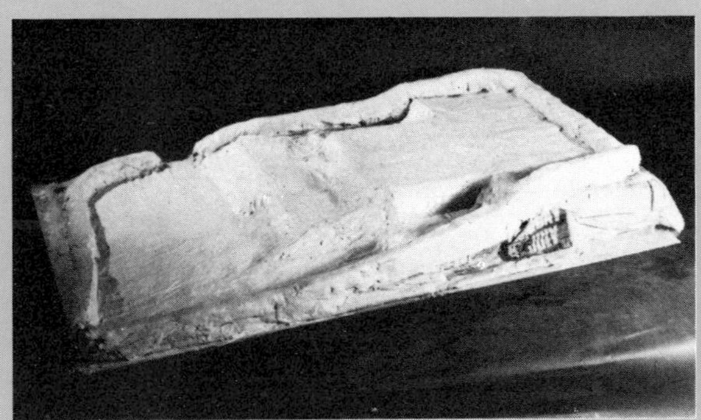

7. . . . like this. Note the gap left for the entrance to the bailey (the name of the area inside the walls).

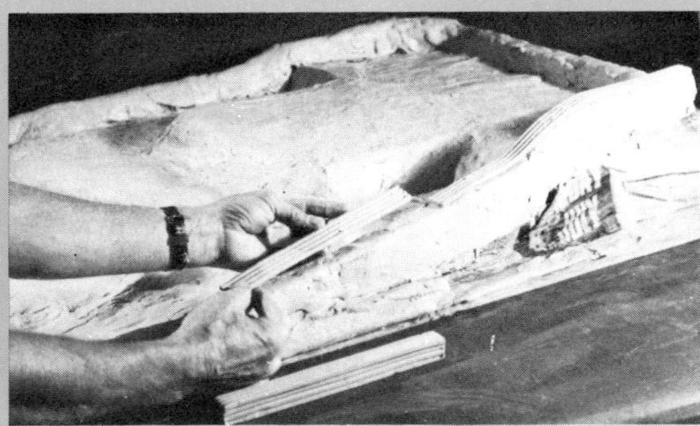

8. Take 2 new packets of Plasticine. Fit strips of Plasticine along the top of the Roman wall.

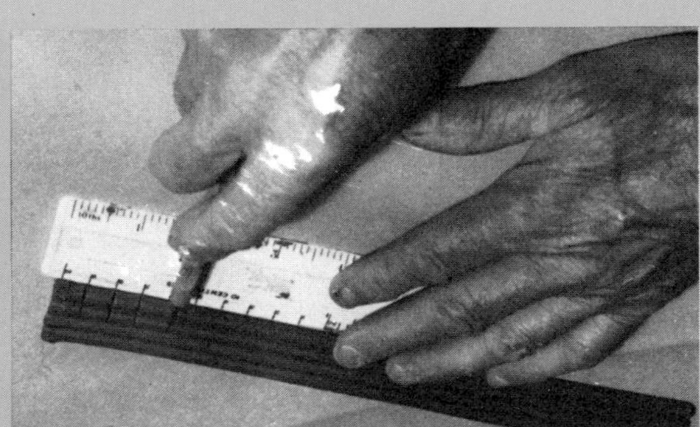

9. Make cuts halfway into a strip of Plasticine 1 cm apart . . .

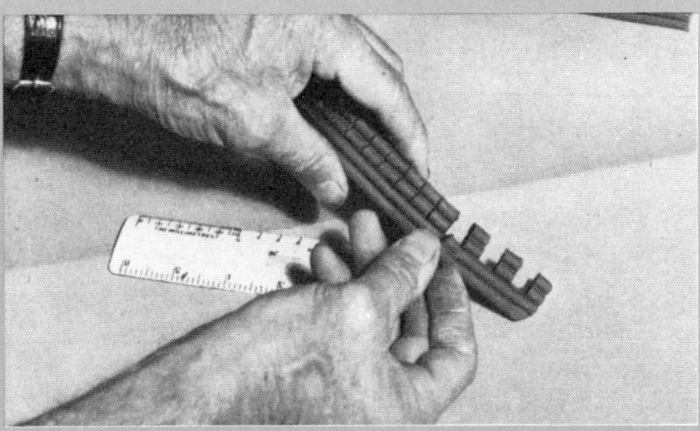

10. . . . and tear out every other section to make battlements . . .

11. . . . to fit round the tops of the walls. The bastions (round towers) are made of rolled-up corrugated paper glued into position.

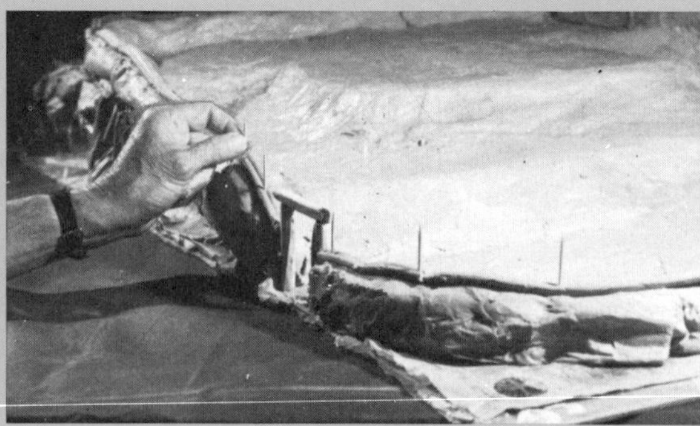

12. Place further strips of Plasticine along the top of the rampart. Take about 12 cocktail sticks, break in half and fit into Plasticine as shown, pointed ends upwards. The entrance gateway is made of corrugated paper rolled-up.

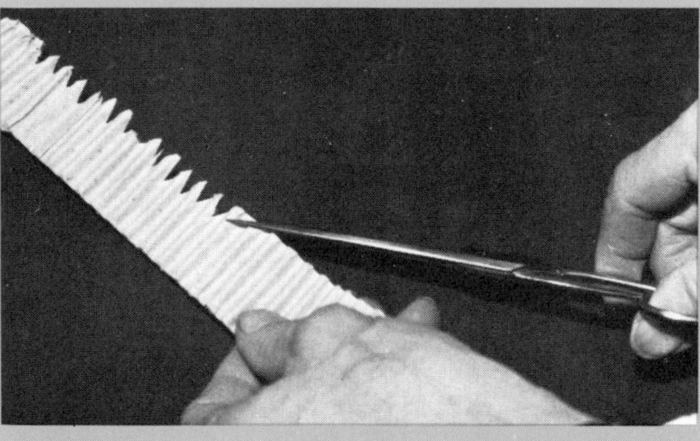

13. Cut strips of corrugated paper 3 cm wide. Use scissors to cut one edge into points. This is the wooden fence or palisade.

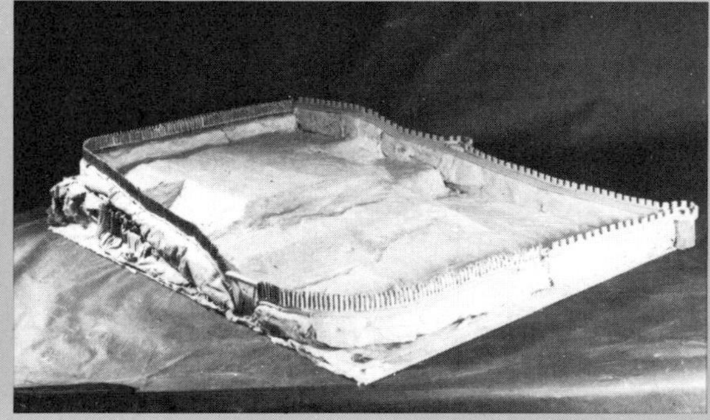

14. Fit it into place over the points of the cocktail sticks.

15. Make holes in the lid of a plastic carton.

16. Half fill the carton with yellow powder paint (dry). Shake a thick layer of powder over the clay. Refill the shaker with blue powder paint and scatter this amongst the yellow powder. Use less blue than yellow.

17. Take a stiff brush (a washing-up brush is best). Use it to stipple the powder into the wet clay to make grass.

18. Find several kinds of moss. Plant them in the clay to act as bushes.

Part 2
The wooden tower

You will need:

cocktail sticks
milk drinking straws
newspapers
corrugated paper
Plasticine
12″ gramophone record

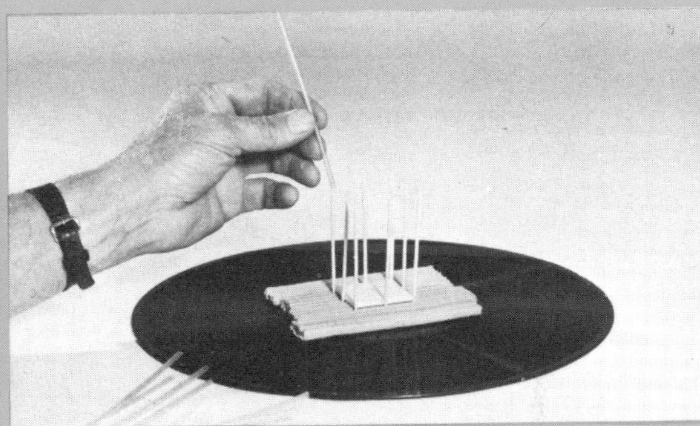

19. Take the record. Lay strips of Plasticine across the middle. Cut a square of card 4 cm × 4 cm. Push 8 cocktail sticks into the Plasticine round the square. Take 8 plastic milk straws and place over the sticks.

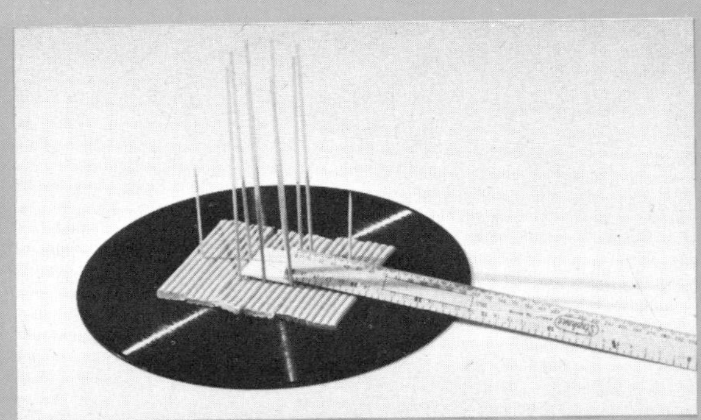

20. Place 2 more cocktail sticks 4 cm away from the square.

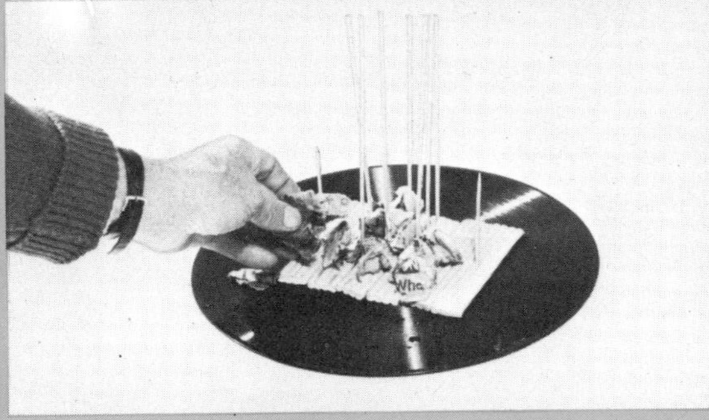

21. Soak some more newspapers. Break them into small pieces and pile them inside and round the uprights.

22. Complete the pile to the top of the cocktail sticks (arrowed).

23. Complete the castle mound and make the frame for the tower. Use more drinking straws and fix them to the uprights with sewing pins.

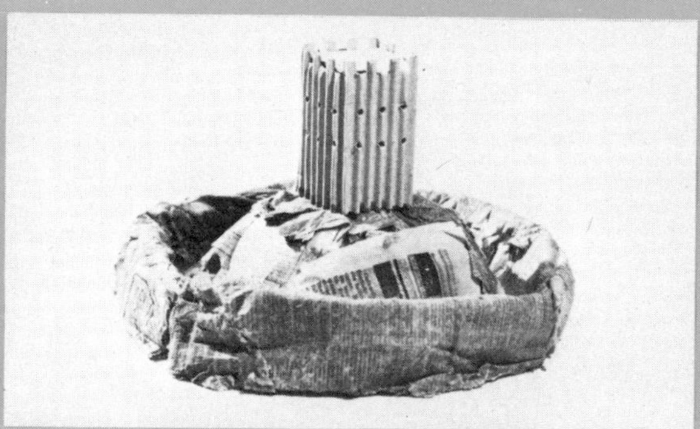

24. Soak more newspapers and roll them up to make the bank round the base of the mound. Cover the tower with corrugated paper.

25. Cover the newspaper with a layer of wet clay.

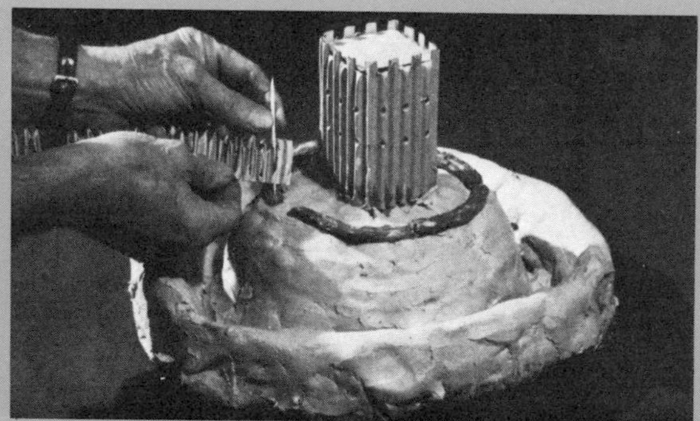

26. Lay a 'snake' of Plasticine round the top of the mound to hold the fence which protects it. Make the fence from corrugated paper as in picture 13. Use cocktail sticks to fix it in place.

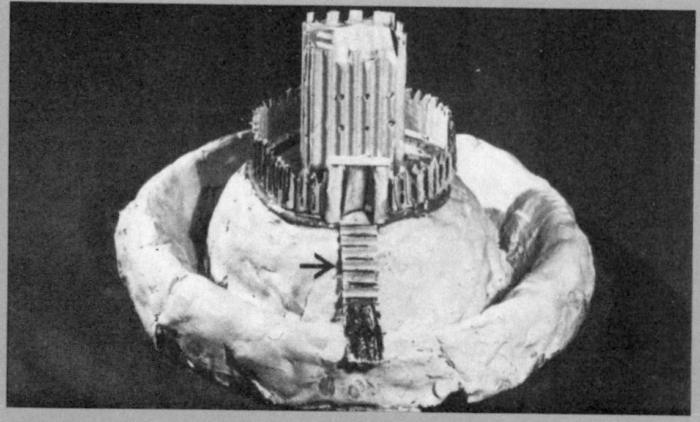

27. Corrugated paper makes a good flight of steps up the mound into the castle (arrowed), and a bridge across the ditch to the steps. The gate is made of card and rolled-up corrugated paper for the posts.

28. Fit the castle into the corner of the bailey. Build the ground up to the top of the bank in front of the ditch using wet newspaper and clay as in pictures 4–7.

29. This is how the 'wooden castle' may have looked when it was built in the corner of the Roman city walls. Nobody really knows exactly where it was built but when you visit the Tower of London you will be able to see for yourself if the place we have chosen was a good one.

2 The Bishop Builds a Tower

Gundulf, Bishop of Rochester, stood on the river bank and looked happily at the busy scene.

'Look sharp then, Tom!' he heard one burly labourer shout to his mate, 'my lord bishop is watching thee. His great tower will not get built by sitting down!'

There were three ships moored nearby and the labourers were unloading stone for the building of King William's Tower of London. Ralph, the master mason in charge of the building, stood beside the bishop, watching as the labourers carried the heavy blocks of stone up the river bank in baskets and laid them in neat piles ready for use. Others were dragging up the larger blocks on sleds.

'We must build up stocks for next year, my lord,' said Ralph. 'The voyage from Normandy can be rough in bad weather and supplies from the quarries at Caen will stop if our ships cannot sail.' The bishop nodded.

The tower was more than half built. There were tall scaffolding poles all round it, and on planks tied to the poles masons were working on the thick strong walls. Labourers were carrying stones and mortar to be hoisted up to them in baskets with ropes and pulleys.

Around the tower was a jumble of huts and sheds. Smoke rose from cooking fires, from a blacksmith's forge and from a fire on which limestone was being burned to make the mortar.

It was a noisy scene with carpenters sawing and hammering, masons cutting stone, blacksmiths beating out iron and the labourers shouting to each other as they carried their heavy loads.

The bishop now led the way up the shaky ladders to the top of the scaffolding, his long black robes flapping around him. 'This tower will not be easily taken, Ralph,' he said, looking down at the ground far below. 'These walls will not be quickly broken by an enemy!'

'No, my lord,' said Ralph, 'nor will prisoners

find an easy escape from the tower.'

'I pray to God there be few such poor creatures shut up in my tower,' said Gundulf. And he turned to more cheerful things.

With his master mason he inspected the work of the stone masons to see that the blocks were laid close together so that neither rain nor frost could get in. He looked carefully at the filling of rubble and mortar that made the thickness of the wall, to see that it was firm and strong. The walls were nearly four metres thick and the two men could easily walk round the top.

Now they came to the part of the castle which gave the bishop special pleasure. This was the Chapel of St John and he wanted it to be the finest chapel in all England. As he looked down on it from the top of the wall he could picture in his mind's eye the paintings and tapestries which would cover the walls behind those beautiful stone columns. He could almost hear the singing which would echo round the fine arches when the services were held. 'You have done well, Ralph,' he said. 'The king will be pleased with your work.'

But even as he spoke, trumpets sounded and a group of horsemen rode towards the castle from the London street nearby.

'The king is coming now,' said Ralph anxiously. 'We shall soon see if he is pleased!' And the two men climbed down from the tower to meet the king.

This was not the King William who had conquered England, for this was the year 1087 and William the Conqueror was dead. The king who now approached with trumpets sounding and flags flying was the Conqueror's son, called William the Red, or 'Rufus', because of his brick red face.

Followed by some of his barons and men-at-arms, he now rode up to the bishop and Ralph. 'What news, good Gundulf?' shouted the king, as he approached. 'How goes my stone castle?'

Bishop Gundulf smiled when he heard the king say *stone* castle. The old wooden castle still stood guard over London. It was only a few metres from where the new tower was being built and it would not be knocked down and the mound cleared until the stone tower was finished.

'It goes well, Your Grace,' replied Gundulf. 'The tower grows daily and within my lifetime, God willing, it shall be finished.'

The king was not pleased by the bishop's reply. 'In your lifetime is it, my lord bishop?' he growled. Then his face darkened. 'That is what holds up my work!' – and he pointed to the rounded wall where St John's Chapel was being built. 'If you did not take such care of your precious chapel, my castle would be finished this very year.'

The bishop paused before he replied. The chapel had been planned with the approval of William the Conqueror who was a religious man. Rufus, his son, was not religious, but it would not pay to make him angry.

'The chapel is my work for God, Sire,' said Gundulf. 'The castle is for Your Grace.'

'God, then, comes first with you!' said the king, his red face colouring almost to purple. 'Your duty to me comes only second – is that it?' Rufus could hardly control his rage. He had no choice but to keep the bishop in charge of the work on the castle for only he, in all England, could finish it now.

Churchmen were almost the only ones among all his subjects who could read and write well enough to take charge of the construction of important buildings. Gundulf, moreover, had seen to the building of churches and monasteries. The Tower of London was easy for him to build as compared with a great cathedral.

But Rufus hated the quiet, superior manner of the smiling bishop.

Then a sudden idea came to the angry king. He smiled grimly. 'My father gave you a fine country estate, did he not, my lord bishop?'

'Yes, Sire,' replied Gundulf. 'Your royal father gave me Haddenham Manor, in Buckinghamshire. The income from the farms is needed for the upkeep of my monastery at Rochester.'

The king smiled. 'And now that I am king, you will want me to let you keep Haddenham, will you not, my lord?'

'Yes indeed, Sire,' said the bishop, wondering what the king was planning.

'Then you shall keep the manor,' the king said. 'For one hundred pounds!'

Gundulf gasped. One hundred pounds was a great deal of money.

'But, Sire,' he began, hoping to persuade the king to change his mind. 'The land was a gift. My poor monks could not afford to buy it from Your Grace.'

'Then I shall have it back,' declared Rufus.

The bishop was also becoming angry, and was just about to speak more roughly to the king when a man came between them. This was Henry, Earl of Warwick, who was one of the king's courtiers.

'Your Grace, there is no cause for a quarrel,' he said. 'Let the good bishop Gundulf, at his own cost, build a strong wall round your castle at Rochester. In return, let him keep the manor.'

The king's anger suddenly turned to laughter. 'You are a clever man, Henry,' he said. 'Rochester castle does indeed need a wall to make it stronger and who better to build it than my lord bishop!' And he turned to Gundulf. 'Build me that wall and the land shall stay with your monks,' he declared.

And that is how matters were arranged. The king's tower was built and so was his wall at Rochester castle, which cost the bishop only forty pounds to build. The monks lived their good lives at the monastery in peace. And so the bishop was able to serve both God and his king.

Things to look at and to do 2

1. At some time people began to call Gundulf's Tower of London the 'White Tower'. This was probably because the stone of the walls was a very pale colour when it was new. It could also have been because later on, when the stone became blackened with soot from the chimneys of London, it was whitewashed to make it look clean again. Can you think of another name for the White Tower?

Colchester Castle

Rochester Castle – Gundulf's wall is on the left of the picture

2. As the story says, the White Tower is the first castle keep in Britain which the Normans built of stone. There are very few other Norman stone keeps in this country but perhaps there is one near your home or where you go on holiday? Maybe you can visit Colchester Castle. Can you tell what has happened to it since the Normans built it? The other Norman keeps you may see will be tall, square ones like Rochester Castle (look carefully at the picture of Rochester Castle and you will see the wall which Bishop Gundulf built for William Rufus), or round, hollow ones – called 'shell keeps' – like the one at Carisbrooke in the Isle of Wight.

Carisbrooke Castle – the shell keep is in the right-hand corner

Chapel of St John

3. Gundulf's chapel is a beautiful example of a Norman church building. The stonework is simple and strong. The round-headed arches, the vaulted ceiling and the apse where the altar is are all typically Norman.

4. You will see two kinds of vaulting. There is tunnel-vaulting over the nave and galleries and groin vaulting over the aisles. (Groin vaulting is made by two tunnel vaults cutting across each other.) The model of the chapel will help you to understand how these arches were built.

5. The stone, from Caen in Normandy, was cut into smooth blocks that fitted together perfectly. This kind of stonework is called 'ashlar'. Compare it with the other walls inside and outside the White Tower which are made of rubble.

6. There is no carving on the stonework, except for simple designs on the capitals at the top of the pillars round the nave. How many different designs can you see? Notice the cross on some of the capitals. This is called a 'Tau' cross (Tau is the Greek letter T), or St Anthony's Cross.

7. The Normans were great builders of cathedrals and churches but very few are as unchanged as the Chapel of St John. When next you visit a cathedral or a church built by the Normans, see how much of the original stonework you can find.

8. Today, the chapel has bare walls and is brightly lit. In Norman times it would have been lit by candles for the windows would have had richly-coloured glass which shut out the daylight. The stone walls would have been painted with holy pictures or hung with tapestries showing scenes from the Bible. Why not paint a picture of the chapel as it might have looked in Norman times? Or write a poem about a service there in Bishop Gundulf's time?

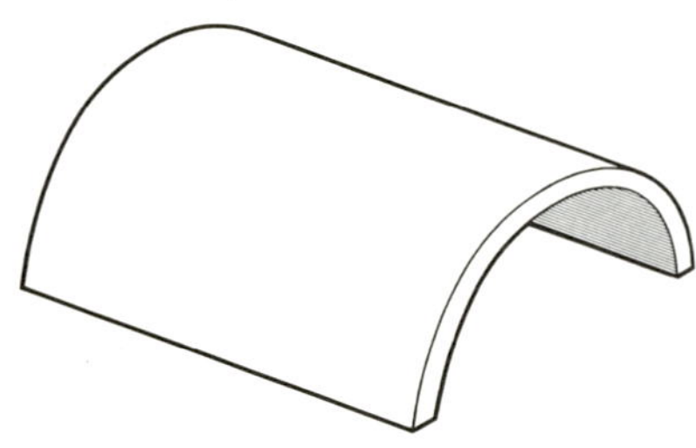

Tunnel vaulting

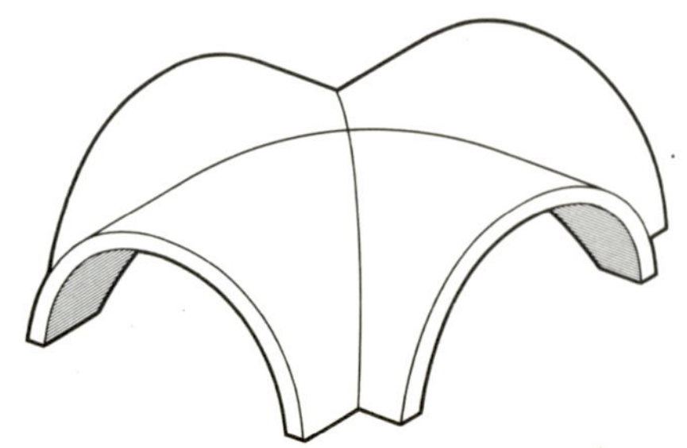

Groin vaulting

Model 2: St John's Chapel

The photographs which follow show you how to make a model of the beautiful Norman chapel inside the White Tower. It fits into the model of the tower as shown on page 27, pictures 1, 2 and 3. If you have not time to make this part of the White Tower, miss it out and use two detergent packets in its place.

You will need:

a length of ½″ dowelling
Plasticine
plastic meat trays
toilet roll inners
a cheese spread packet
corrugated paper

1. Take 2 Eurosize 3 detergent packets. Cut them both open like this.

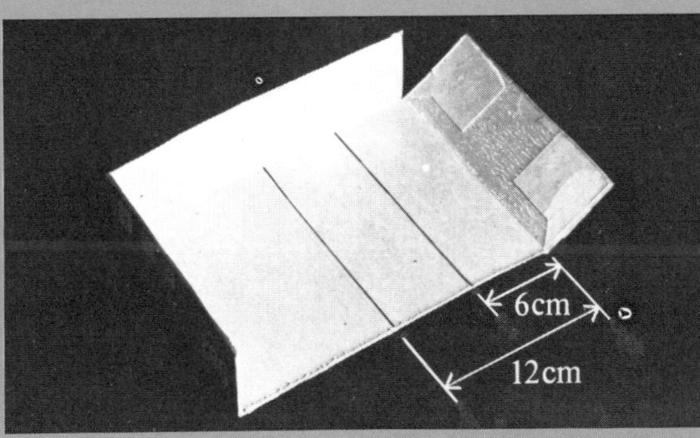

2. Take one of them and cut down one corner so that the end flap can be folded back. Draw lines as shown.

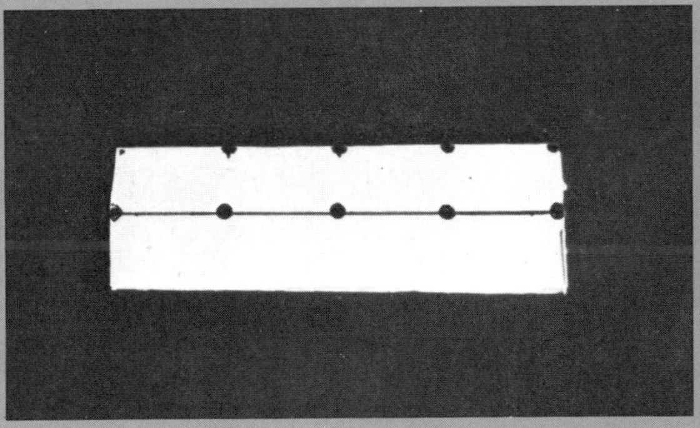

3. Cut a piece of thick card 16 cm × 8 cm. Mark it like this.

4. Glue it into place as the floor of one side of the chapel.

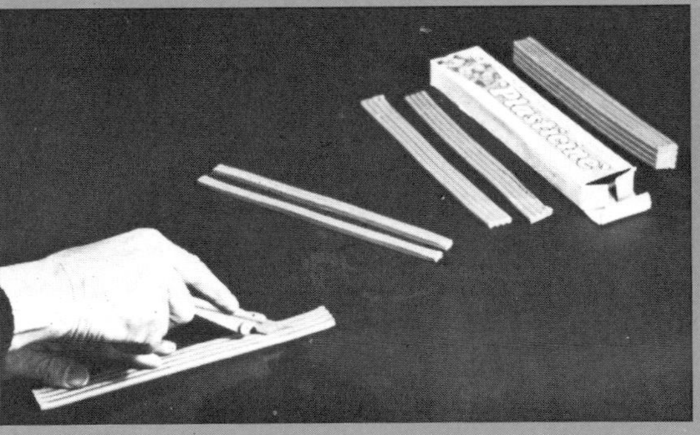

5. Take a new packet of Plasticine. Cut strips two and three corrugations wide.

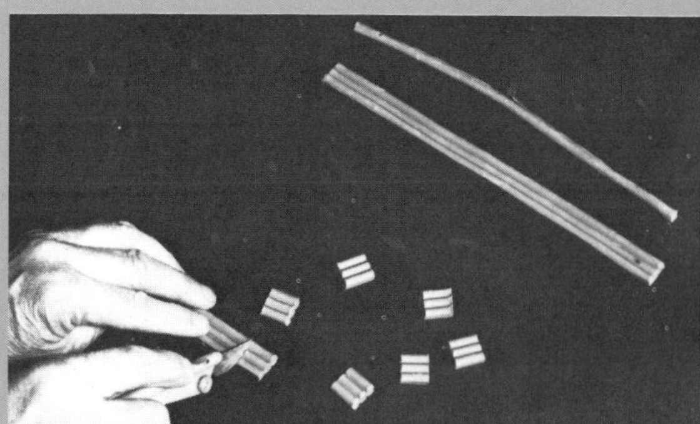

6. Cut squares from the 3 corrugation strips. Cut 24 squares.

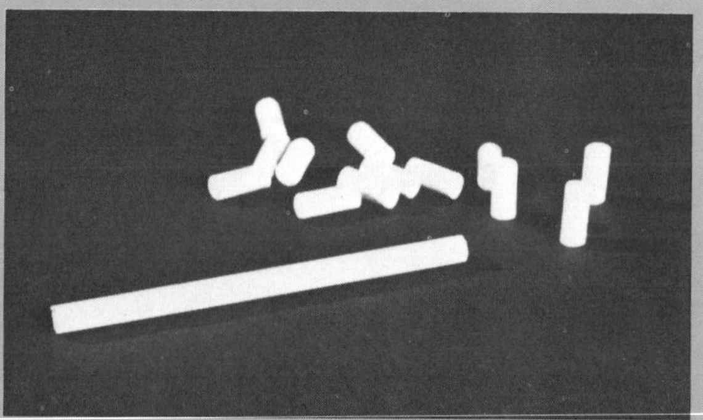

7. Take a length of $\frac{1}{2}$″ dowelling. Use a saw to cut 3 cm sections. Cut 12 of them. These are the columns for the chapel.

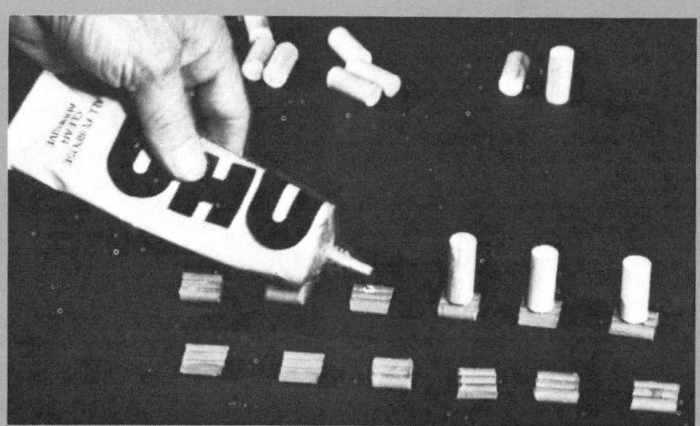

8. Glue each to a Plasticine square . . .

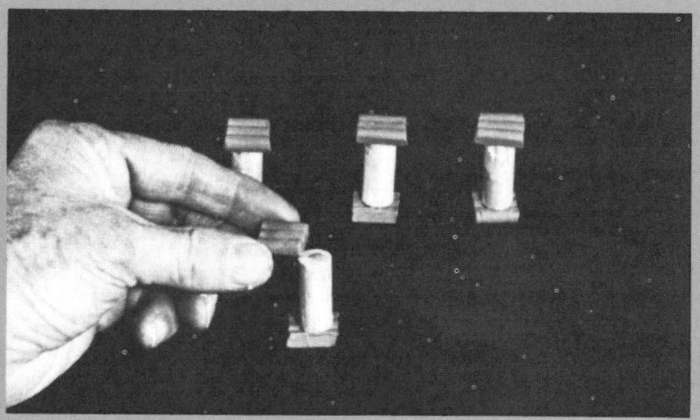

9. . . . and glue another square on top. The columns now have bases and capitals.

10. Cut 4 two-corrugation wide lengths of Plasticine, 3·5 cm long, and glue them against the wall at each mark. Glue a half-square of Plasticine on top of each. The corner pillar (arrowed) is one-corrugation wide.

11. Stand four of the columns on their floor marks and cut four 5 cm lengths of single-corrugation Plasticine for arches against the back wall. Glue the arches into position.

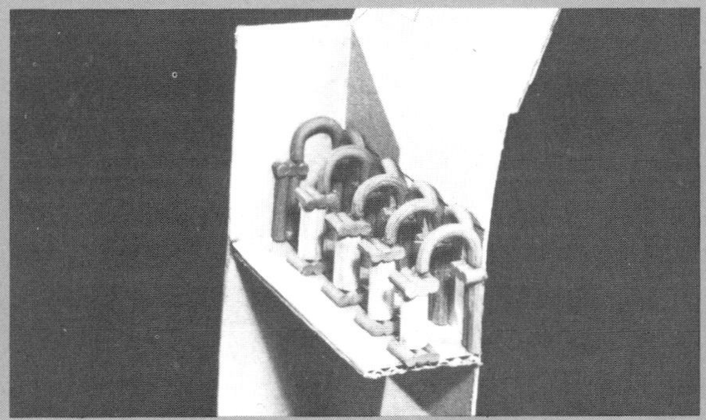

12. Make five more 5 cm arches and glue them into position like this. Notice the end column at the back.

13. Four arches are glued into place between the columns. Cut an 11·5 cm length of dowelling to support the floor (arrowed).

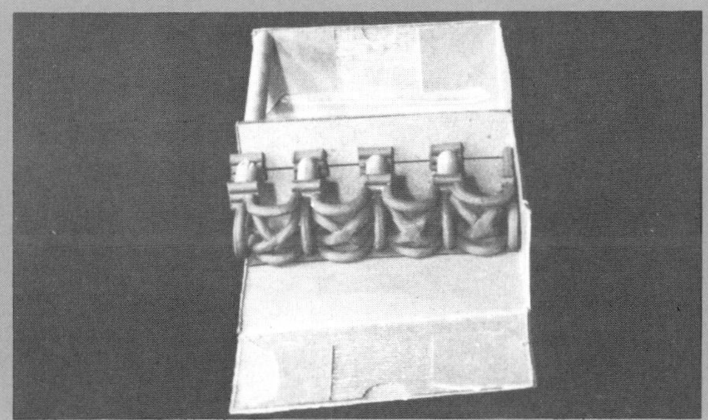

14. Fit more Plasticine arches across the bays and glue them into position.

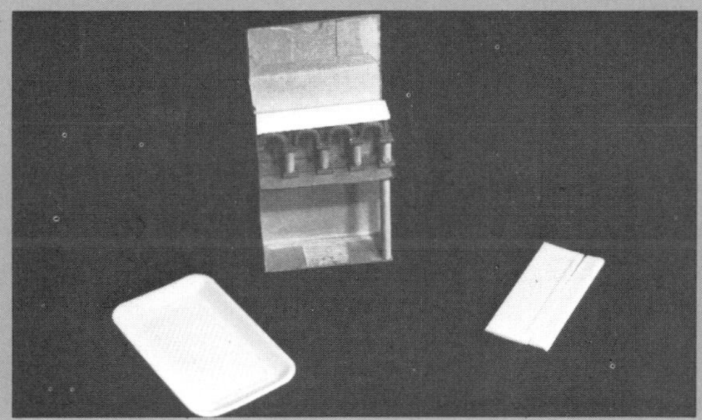

15. Take a plastic meat tray (a thin sheet of card will do instead) and cut sections to fit on top of the arches . . .

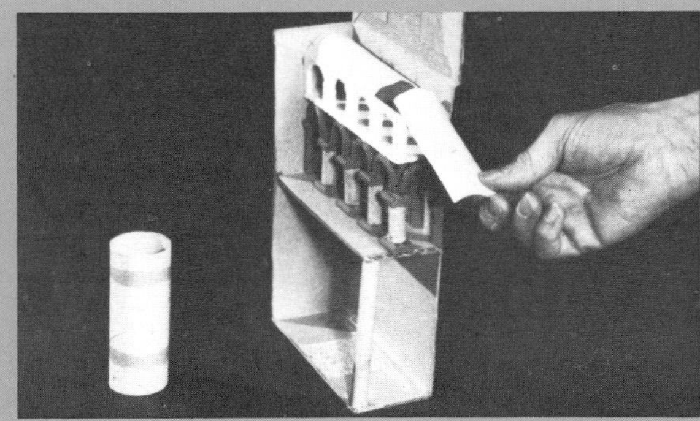

16. . . . to make the upper floor of the chapel. The roof is made from 2 toilet roll inners.

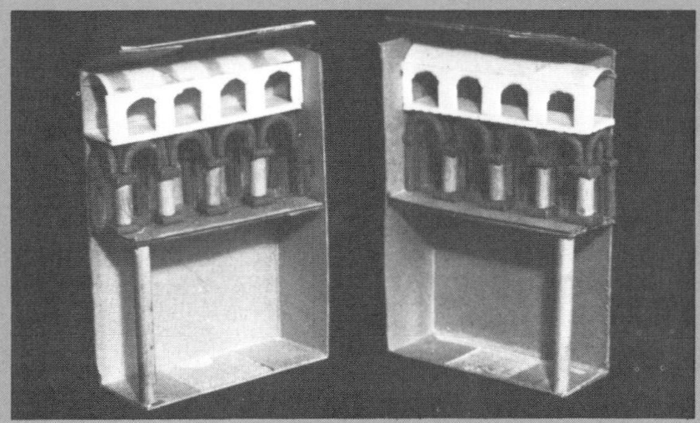

17. The other half of the chapel should now be finished.

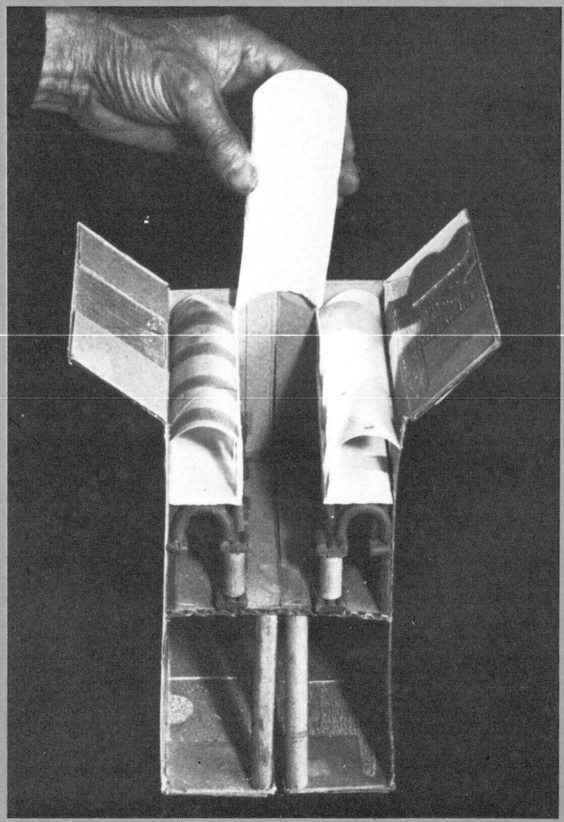

18. The two halves can now be fitted together and a roof (this one is cut from a plastic meat tray) fitted between them.

19. The apse (curved end) of the chapel is made from an empty cheese spread packet and a sheet of corrugated paper 19 cm × 24 cm.

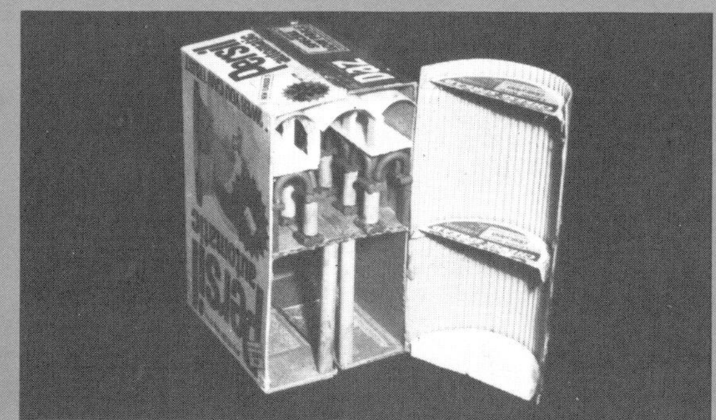

20. The lid and base of the carton are cut in half and the corrugated paper is glued round them, to fit the floor and ceiling levels of the chapel.

21. Cut a section of corrugated paper to fit over the floor. Mark it for the columns like this.

22. Fit the floor into position and make wall columns as for the chapel.

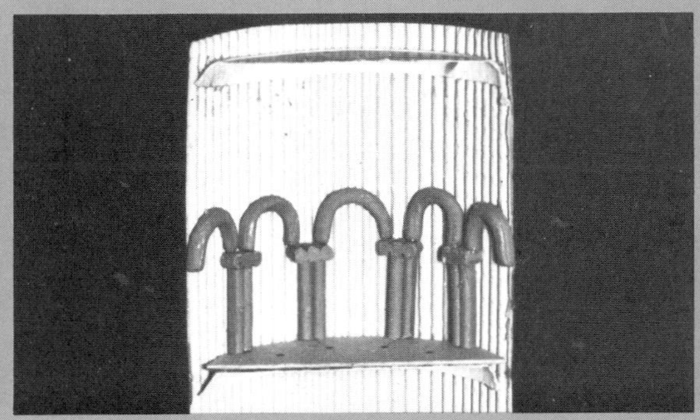

23. Glue arches into position . . .

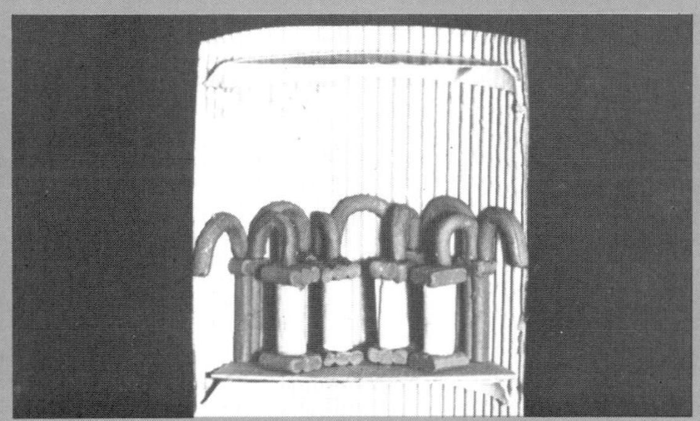

24. . . . and the four columns . . .

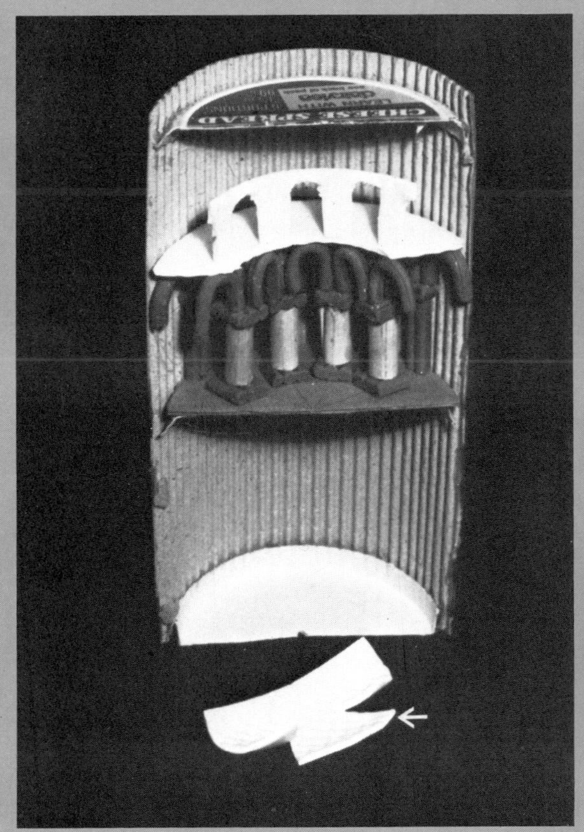

25. . . . use a plastic meat tray for the gallery and arches and use another section of meat tray to make the domed ceiling (arrowed) . . .

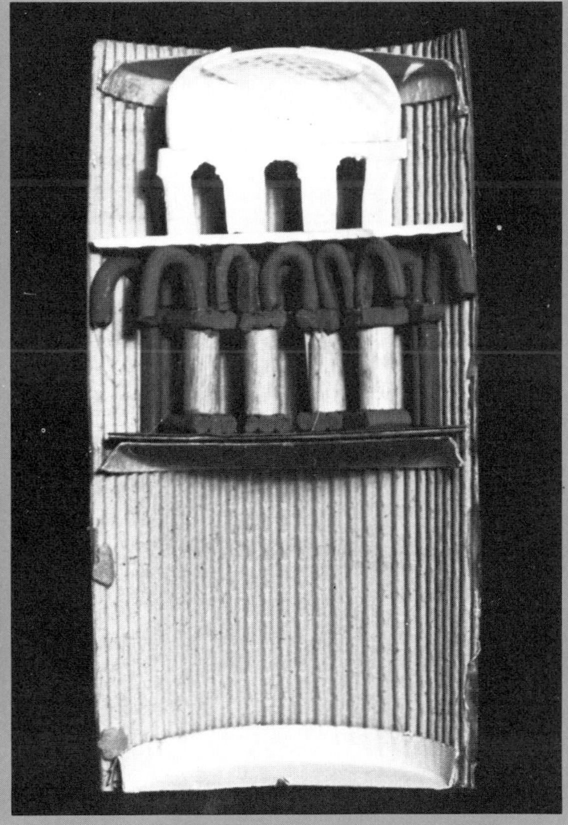

26. . . . which fits into place like this. See pictures 20 and 21 of the next chapter to see how the apse fits the front of the chapel.

3 Escape from the Tower

Great preparations were being made in Bishop Gundulf's tower. The royal apartments on the upper floor were being decorated with fine new tapestries on the walls. The cellar was being stocked with choice wines and there was even new furniture in the royal bedroom. But Sir John, the captain of the guard, was not at all pleased.

'Anyone would think that His Holiness the Pope was coming to live here!' he grumbled. 'All this good money being spent on a mere prisoner!'

'Ranulf Flambard is no common prisoner, John,' one of the other knights told him. 'He is rich!'

'Aye,' added another, 'Flambard is richer than King Henry himself and a rich prisoner can buy himself comfort and luxury – even in the Tower of London!'

'He is an upstart priest,' grumbled Sir John, 'who wheedled his way into the king's favour. He can go hang for all I care!'

What they said was true, for King William Rufus had made Ranulf one of his ministers with the task of raising money from taxes. He had, moreover, been so successful that the royal treasury was filled with money. But nobody likes paying taxes, and the more money Ranulf collected from the people the more they hated him. They called him 'Flambard' which is French for 'firebrand' because people said that his taxes ate up their money like a fierce flame.

When William Rufus died, his brother Henry became king. Rufus had been very unpopular and Henry wanted to be liked by the people. He promised not to behave as badly as his brother and to prove his good intentions he had Ranulf arrested.

Kings need money, however, and Henry knew that, one day, he might need Flambard to raise money for him. It would pay to treat him well in prison, and as Henry had other castles where he preferred to live, he decided that Flambard should be made comfortable during his imprisonment in the royal apartments in the Tower.

No wonder that Sir John and the other knights were angry. They had expected that Ranulf would at last be made to pay for his pride and greed, but instead he was still living in luxury.

It was not long, however, before Sir John and his friends changed their minds. No sooner had Ranulf moved into the upper floor of the Tower than he began to make friends with everybody. He was allowed to bring his own servants with him and these cooked his food in the kitchens in the bailey. They looked after all his needs, bringing him wine from the cellars and keeping a fire burning in his apartments, for it was winter and very cold in London.

The Tower guards soon found that they were getting a share of Ranulf's luxuries for they were given all the food left over from his rich meals and a share of his wine as well. They began to like their fat, cheerful prisoner and it was not long before they were laughing and joking with him, sometimes even sitting with him in the evenings when they were on guard, enjoying jugs of wine and listening to him tell of the days when he was the king's minister.

One cold night in February of the year 1101, Ranulf was especially friendly to his guards. He chatted happily and shared jug after jug of wine with them. 'Come, my friends,' he would say, beckoning to his servant to bring yet another jug, 'drink to my health, for it is not healthy to be shut up in a tower like this without sunshine or fresh air.' And his friendly guards lifted their cups and pledged: 'A good health to your honour', as they drank deeply. They did not notice, however, that for every four cups of wine they drank, Ranulf drank less than one. Soon the guards began to feel sleepy as the wine went to their heads. And it was not long before they were all snoring gently with half-filled wine cups in their hands and their heads resting on the table.

'To the cellars,' Ranulf told his servants, and as they went down to where the wine was kept, the guards on the winding stairs laughed at them: 'What! Going to fetch more wine?' they called. 'His lordship will be drunk this night!' And they let them pass.

In the cellars the servants went to one particular cask which they now carefully carried back to the royal apartments. There they quickly opened the top and coiled inside was a long rope!

'Tie one end to the stone bar in the middle of that window,' ordered Ranulf. Then, as they did as he told them, letting the rope out so that it hung down outside the high wall of the Tower, Ranulf got ready for his escape.

It was a cold night so he put on warm clothes. Then helped by his servants, he climbed out of the window more than twenty metres above the ground, and grasped the rope tightly with both hands.

It was a pity that Ranulf had enjoyed his luxuries so much for his good meals had made him fat and heavy. He began to slide down the rope. He gripped it tightly but it slipped through his hands, cutting and burning them as he dropped faster and faster towards the ground below. Desperately he managed to slow down his fall. But then, when he was almost at the bottom of the wall – he came to the end of the rope! It was too short and Ranulf fell the last two metres with a heavy bump. He was badly bruised and his hands were burned and bleeding. But he was out of the Tower!

There were still the outer walls to cross however and how he managed to get through the bailey and out of the heavily guarded gate is still a secret which only he and his servants knew. Maybe the guards on the walls were also drunk on their prisoner's wine; or were they, perhaps, paid money to let him through?

Somehow Ranulf did manage to escape from the bailey and by dawn he was safely on board a ship bound for Normandy.

He was the first prisoner we know of to be kept in the Tower – and the first to escape from it.

Things to look at and to do 3

1. The White Tower was built as a palace and fortress but it could also be a strong prison. It was as hard for a prisoner to get out as it was for an enemy to get in. There was only one doorway which was high above the ground. This is the door through which you go into the White Tower now. The wooden staircase leading up to it is like the one the Normans had.

Why was the entrance so far above the ground?

The large windows in the White Tower were put in only about two hundred and fifty years ago. In medieval times there were proper windows at the top, but much smaller openings lower down. Can you guess why they were made smaller?

The walls were much too thick to break through. You can see how thick they were from the window openings. Measure one when you visit the White Tower.

There was only one staircase inside the White Tower which went from the bottom to the top. This made it easy to stop an enemy who had got into the entrance floor from getting any higher, or to catch a prisoner trying to escape from the top of the Tower. You go down this staircase when you leave the top floor during your tour. What kind of staircase is it and which turret is it in?

2. Ranulf Flambard avoided all these problems by climbing down from one of the windows at the top of the Tower using a long rope. Can you think of any other way in which he could have escaped?

3. The only windows in the White Tower which are still as they were in Ranulf's time are at the top left of the south face. It is said that the one from which Ranulf escaped is the left-hand one nearest to the turret (see page 26).

4. The entrance floor where Ranulf's guards lived now contains the Sporting Gallery and the Tournament Gallery; look to your right just

Section of a wall in the White Tower

Staircase in the White Tower

South face of the White Tower

after you enter the Sporting Gallery and you will see the head of a wild animal and the spears used to hunt it. This animal's head was often served whole at medieval banquets. Probably Ranulf's rich meals in the Tower would have included it. What is the animal? Why are there bars on the hunting spears?

5. When Ranulf was a prisoner, the Constable of the Tower was William de Mandeville, the father of Geoffrey whom you will read about in the next chapter. King Henry suspected that William had allowed Ranulf to escape, and for that reason he dismissed him from his post as Constable of the Tower. Supposing you were King Henry, what would have made you suspicious of William de Mandeville? How could William have defended himself from the charge against him? You could write a story or a play about it.

Model 3: The White Tower

Part 1
The walls

You will need:

8 Eurosize 3 detergent packets
a strip of corrugated paper 123cm × 25cm

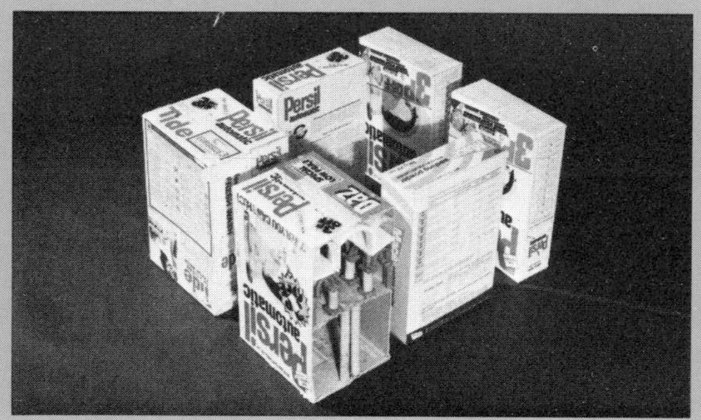

1. Take 8 Eurosize 3 detergent packets. (If you have made St John's Chapel, this will count as two of the packets.) Arrange them as shown.

2. Fix them together with glue and sticky tape. Mark the North, South, East and West points as shown. This will be a scale model of the White Tower in centimetres (1 cm=1 metre).

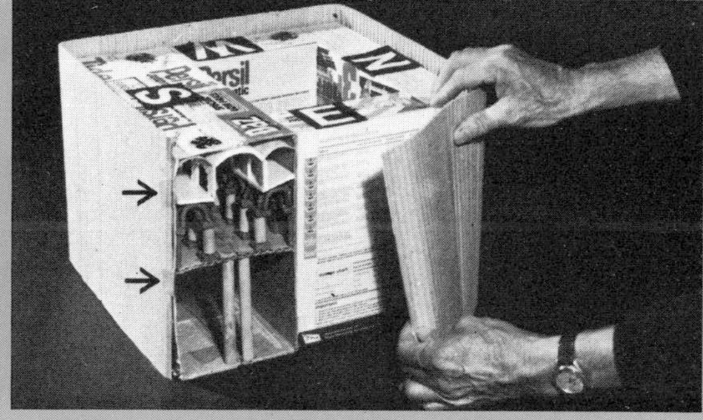

3. Cut a strip of corrugated paper 123 cm long and 25 cm wide. Fix one end with sticky tape (arrowed) and fit the rest round the packets, making folds at each corner.

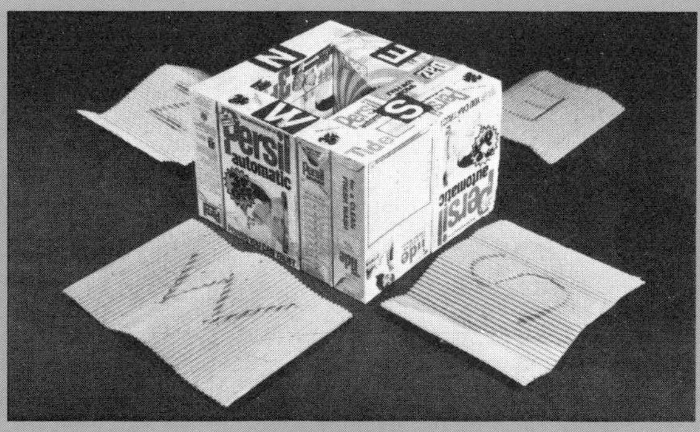

4. Cut the corrugated paper along each corner fold. Mark the compass points on the back of each to match the walls they fit.

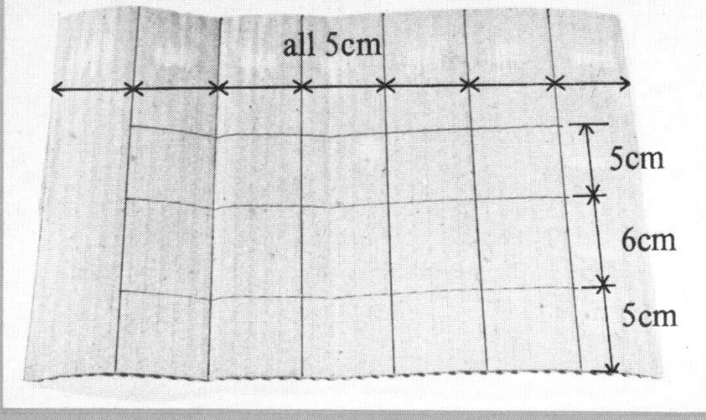

5. Make this pattern. It is a template for the buttresses and windows.

6. Draw the lines on each wall, like this.

Part 2
The buttresses and windows

You will need:

2 packets of Plasticine
white chalk and black crayon

7. Take a new packet of Plasticine. Cut a strip in half lengthways. Use a short length of ½″ dowelling rod as a rolling pin (a pencil will do but is not as good). Roll the Plasticine strips until they are 1·5 cm wide.

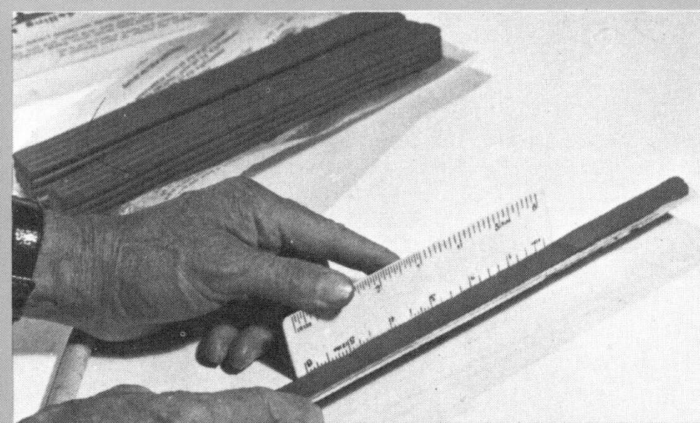

8. Use 2 rulers to straighten the edges. (Press them together.)

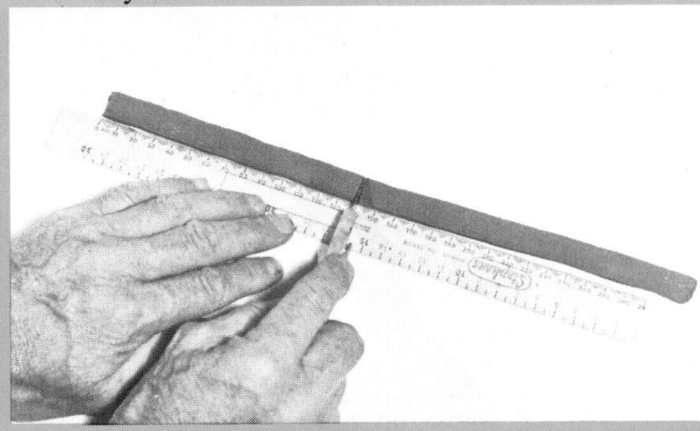

9. Cut off 14 cm lengths. Cut 4 lengths for each wall of the tower.

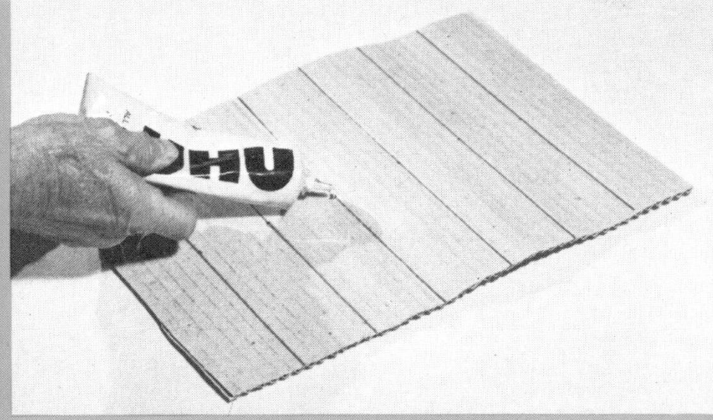

10. Smear glue thinly down each line on one of the walls.

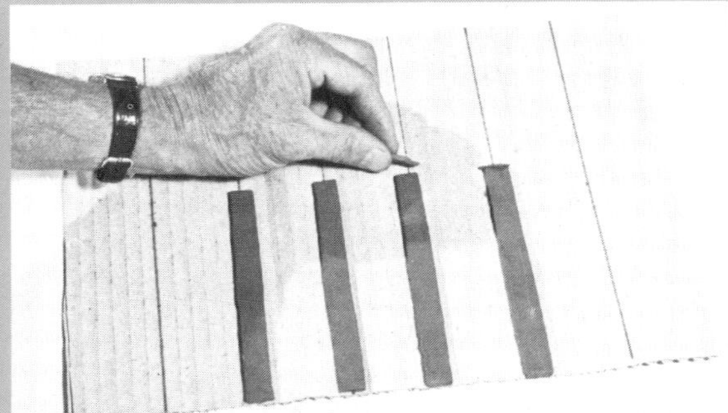

11. Place the strips of Plasticine in position along the glued lines. The caps for the buttresses are made from small pieces of Plasticine.

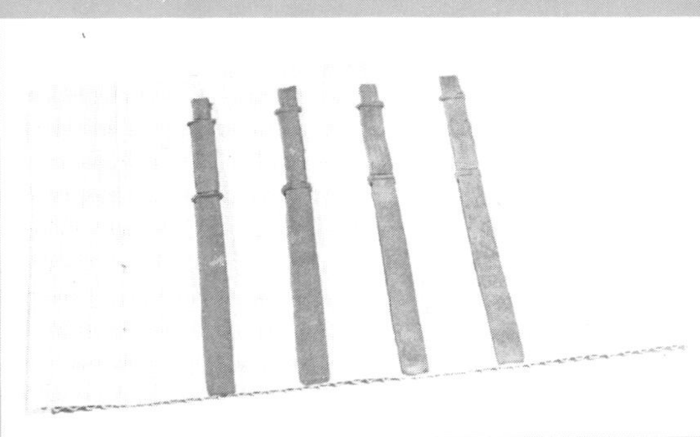

12. Finish the buttresses like this.

13. Make the windows by pressing the edge of a medium-size screwdriver into the corrugated paper . . .

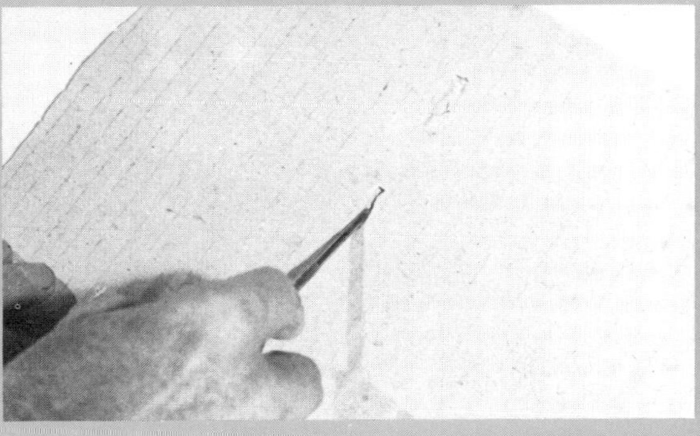

14. . . . and make the arrow slits with a small-size screwdriver.

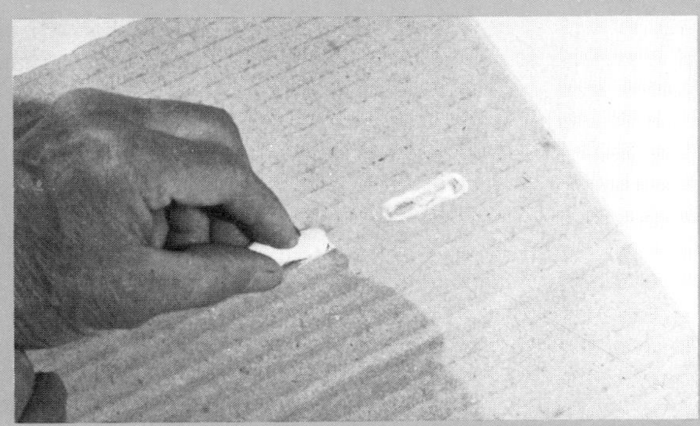

15. Use a piece of white blackboard chalk to outline the windows and slits . . .

16. . . . and a black crayon sharpened to a point to make the shadow in the window spaces.

Part 3
Putting it together

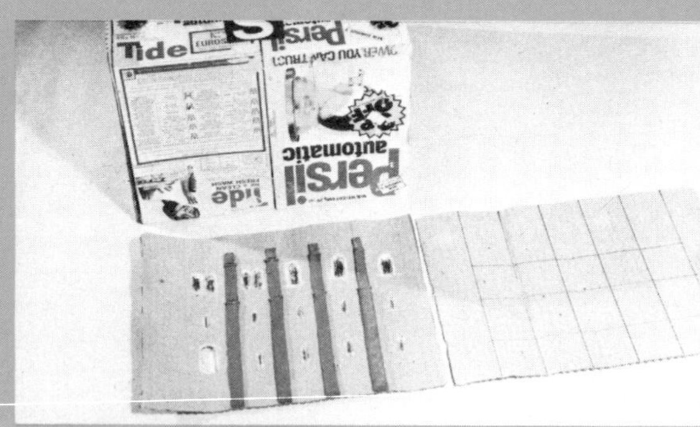

17. Make the south wall like this.

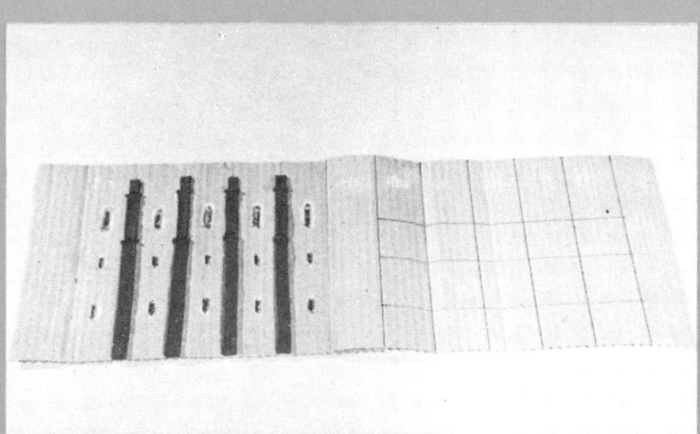

18. Make the west wall like this.

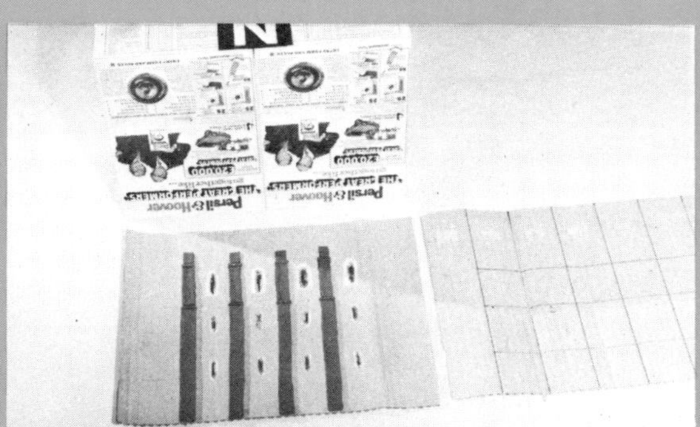

19. Make the north wall like this.

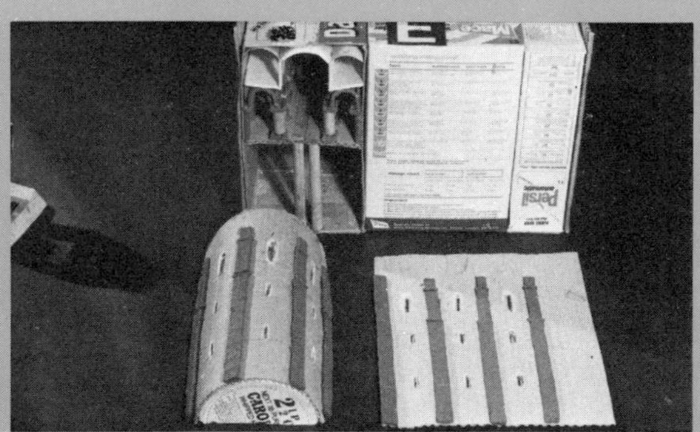

20. Make the east wall and the wall of the chapel like this.

21. This is how it looks when all four walls are completed and glued into place. It is probably as much as had been built when King William Rufus visited it.

4 The Princess in the Tower

Once upon a time, in the kingdom of France, there lived a beautiful princess. Her name was Constance and she lived in a royal palace with her brother who was the king of France. One day, when Constance was about ten years old, her brother called for her and said:

'The time has come, sister, for you to be wed. The king and queen of England have asked for your hand in marriage with their son, Prince Eustace. He is twelve years old and will one day be king of England in his father's place and you will be queen of England. I have decided that it would be an excellent match.'

In those days (it was the year 1140) very young girls might be married to boys of similar age. It was a way of joining families together in peace and friendship, but the children did not live together as husband and wife until they were grown up.

So when she heard the king's words, the princess simply said: 'If it is your wish, I shall obey, Your Grace.' Then she went off to her room in the palace to be by herself and to wonder what it would be like to live in England, and whether Prince Eustace would be brave and handsome (for she had never seen him in all her life), and a thousand other things that a princess thinks about when she is to marry a prince.

And so it happened that Princess Constance was married to Prince Eustace and the bells rang out in joy at the joining of the royal families of England and France.

Matilda, the queen of England, brought Prince Eustace to the wedding and the joy of feasting went on for many days. After the wedding the princess and her prince sat side by side and the courtiers paid compliments to them saying such things as:

'What a fine pair they make!' and, 'There never was a more handsome groom nor a more beautiful bride!'

But it was soon over and her brother, the king of France, came to say goodbye to his sister before she left to live in England.

'You must be brave,' he told her. 'For there is war in England and until it is over you may have to face many dangers. But now Queen Matilda will take you to a safe place in England.' And he kissed her on both cheeks and wished her farewell.

'Farewell, my dear brother,' said Princess Constance. 'I shall try to be brave.'

And so Queen Matilda and the princess, with servants and soldiers, travelled from France and crossed the sea by ship to Dover. On the way, Constance asked the queen about the war in England.

'King Stephen, my husband, became king of England when his uncle, King Henry, died,' the queen explained. 'But King Henry had a daughter named Maud who believed that she should have become queen when her father died. She is trying to turn King Stephen off the throne and there are some powerful barons in England who have taken her side.'

'Can Maud fight against the king of England?' asked Constance.

'She is called the 'Empress Maud',' the Queen corrected her, 'for she was once married to an emperor.' She smiled. 'The empress is very proud. She would not like to be called plain Maud!'

Then the queen became more serious.

'But until the battles are won,' she told Constance, 'we must live in a safe place. And the safest place in England is a fine castle called the Tower of London. That is where we shall go until there is peace in England once more.'

And so the queen and the beautiful princess arrived at the Tower of London and they lived in the royal apartments at the top of the great stone keep – the White Tower.

There were soldiers to defend the castle

and at the head of these there was a rich nobleman named Geoffrey de Mandeville, Earl of Essex. The king had made him Constable of the Tower as a reward for his loyalty and support. At first the earl was kind to the little princess and friendly to the queen. But this was soon to change.

Princess Constance had not seen Prince Eustace since the wedding for after the ceremony he had gone straight back to England. Now, with King Stephen his father, the prince paid a visit to the Tower. Princess Constance could not help being disappointed for the prince talked of nothing but the war with the Empress Maud and seemed not in the least interested in her.

'He is only a boy,' Princess Constance told herself. 'He will change when he grows up to be a man,' and she quickly forgot her disappointment. She liked King Stephen far more than the prince. The king was kind and cheerful. He even played games with her while Prince Eustace looked on. She was sad when the time came for them to leave.

'A king has many duties, my dear,' King Stephen told her as he said goodbye. 'I have enemies and must fight to bring peace to England.'

It was several weeks before news came from the king. And then the news was bad. A great battle had been fought at Lincoln and King Stephen was a prisoner. He had been handed over to the Empress Maud and it was said that she was coming to London to claim the throne. It seemed to Princess Constance that all was lost and that she would never live to be a wife to her prince.

Queen Matilda, however, had a plan. 'I do not trust Geoffrey de Mandeville,' she told Constance. 'I believe that he will betray us. But there are many powerful barons still loyal to the king and my duty now is to lead them

against the empress. You must come with me.'

Geoffrey de Mandeville raised many objections when they told him of their plans.

'It would not be safe for you to travel alone,' he told them. 'Nor can I send soldiers to defend you because I need them here to hold the Tower for the king.'

At last, however, the queen persuaded him that he had no right to prevent her from leaving for she was the lawful ruler of England now that the king was in prison.

So it was that Queen Matilda went off to raise an army and the little princess was left alone with Geoffrey de Mandeville in the Tower of London – for he would not let her go.

It was lonely being the only child in such a great castle and there was little comfort inside Gundulf's strong tower. It was cold and damp, but so were most ordinary houses in those days. The royal apartments she thought were very grand indeed; the great hall with its high walls and its timbered ceiling which reached to the very roof of the Tower; the royal audience chamber where there were thrones for the king and queen when they received visitors; the withdrawing room and, of course, the Chapel of St John where she prayed for the queen to return safely with her army to rescue the king.

At first Constance was allowed to wander freely, talking to the servants as they went about their work and playing games by herself in the great empty rooms. There was a gallery inside the Tower where Constance often walked. It was high up in the walls and ran round all four sides. There were windows along it (one was the window from which Ranulf had made his escape) and Constance often stopped to watch the servants and soldiers in the bailey below.

There were many small buildings in the space within the outer walls. There were stables for horses, workshops where armour and weapons were made and repaired, dovecotes and

chicken coops, a kitchen and a bakery from which there often came a lovely smell of freshly baking bread. It was a busy scene but the little princess often gazed beyond it, across the river to the countryside beyond.

'Will Queen Matilda ever return?' she asked herself. 'Will she ever come to rescue me from the Tower?'

As the weeks passed and no news came, Geoffrey de Mandeville became stricter with Constance. She was soon not allowed out of her room and it was clear that the Constable of the Tower had changed sides. He was now holding the castle, not for King Stephen but for the Empress Maud as Queen of England. Princess Constance was no longer under his protection – she was now his prisoner!

The little prisoner in the Tower was very unhappy as she passed the long hours alone. But one day she heard cheers and shouting outside, and news came that Queen Matilda had returned at the head of a great army. She was approaching London and already houses on the other side of the river were in flames as her army started its attack.

The battle was soon over, for when the people of London saw the smoke rising in the distance they quickly decided to support Queen Matilda. For a time Geoffrey de Mandeville held out against the people of London and Queen Matilda's barons. The Tower was surrounded and from a dark little room Constance could hear the soldiers preparing to defend the Tower. But soon even Geoffrey de Mandeville could see that the empress could never rule England and he opened the gates of the Tower. He led his men out and joined forces with Queen Matilda's victorious army, and Princess Constance was set free.

Soon afterwards, Queen Matilda's soldiers captured the Earl of Gloucester who was the Empress Maud's half brother, and the empress was forced to free King Stephen in exchange for the earl.

So the little princess was rescued and returned to her prince, and the king and queen were reunited. In all the best fairy tales they would have lived happily ever after, but this is a real story about real people and real life does not always have happy endings.

Princess Constance became a wife to Prince Eustace but they were not happy together. The prince died when he was still a young man so he never became king and the little princess never became queen of England. Geoffrey de Mandeville, a traitor to his king, became an outlaw. Later, he was killed attacking one of King Stephen's castles.

Princess Constance did, in the end, live happily ever after, for she married Raymond, the Count of Toulouse, and had a daughter and three sons.

And the Tower of London? Well, Queen Matilda was proved right. It *was* the safest place in England in 1141!

Things to look at and to do 4

1. The great hall is now the Sixteenth Century Gallery and the king's chamber is now the Medieval Gallery. The king's chamber would have been made into separate rooms with screens and curtains; some of these were the private apartments of the king and queen; others were audience chambers where the king heard disputes and talked with his councillors.

In the early days of the White Tower there were only two floors, the entrance floor and this upper floor. The third floor was put in later. Before this, the great hall and chambers went up to the roof as the Chapel of St John still does.

2. How many fireplaces can you find in the White Tower? The smoke was meant to escape through the shafts above them but all too often it blew into the room. One advantage of a high ceiling was that it allowed the smoke to drift up above people's heads.

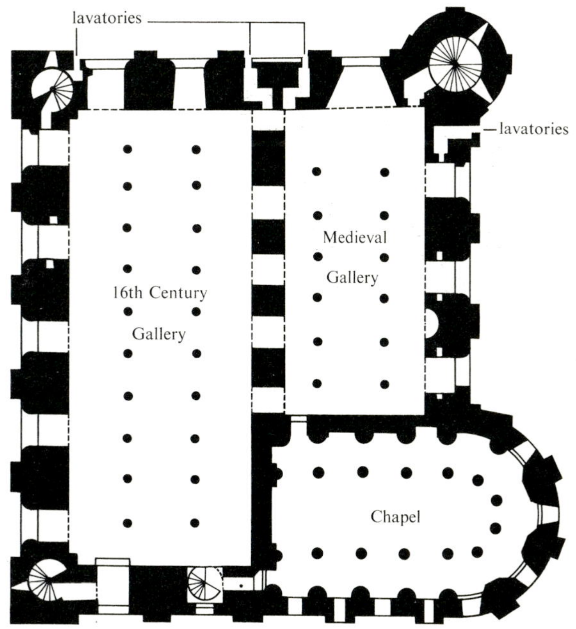

3. There were also small rooms inside the walls, including lavatories. Most of these rooms disappeared when the large windows you see now were put in. But some are left. Go to the far end of the Medieval Gallery and look into the last window opening and along the end wall. Look along the same wall in the Sixteenth Century Gallery, and as you leave it go up the stairs, look to your right and you will see one of the old lavatories with a shaft with daylight at the end of it.

When you are outside the White Tower in front of the Waterloo Building, look up and below the windows of the first floor you will see the ends of chutes from the lavatories.

4. As you go in and out of the Tudor and Seventeenth Century Galleries on the top floor you will walk along part of the gallery which ran right round the Tower, inside the wall. (This is where Princess Constance walked in the story.)

When you are in the Chapel of St John you will see part of the same gallery above the arches. There is a picture of it on page 16. (Perhaps you made the gallery in the model of the Chapel). The king and queen would worship there while everybody else was in the Chapel below them.

North face of the White Tower showing chute exits

Gallery on the top floor

5. As you go into the Medieval Gallery you see shirts of mail. Knights wore shirts of mail like these until about 1400 (after 1300 there were metal plates on top of the mail), when they began to wear suits of plate armour. Many of the soldiers in the stories would have worn mail.

A soldier takes off his mail shirt

Look carefully and you will see that mail is made of metal rings. Each ring has several other rings linked to it. Can you see how many?

6. Queen Matilda, the brave wife of King Stephen, was very religious and she gave money for a hospital to be built near the Tower. It was called the Hospital of St Katharine-by-the-Tower. Why do you think that the hospital was built outside the city walls?

St Katharine's Hospital was pulled down about one hundred and fifty years ago to make way for the docks, which you can see today. A tomb from the old hospital chapel is now in the Chapel of St Peter ad Vincula in the Tower. It is the tomb of the Duke of Exeter who died in 1447. He was once Constable of the Tower. The stone figures of the duke and two of his wives lie under a stone canopy. The tomb is an example of the finest medieval stone carving.

The Exeter tomb

7. Constance would have been taught to read and write as the daughters of kings and nobles (but not many other girls) were in those days. Imagine you are the princess writing to your brother, King Louis of France. Tell him about your first arrival at the Tower of London and then about being kept prisoner there.

Model 4: The White Tower

You will need:

2 large size cooking foil packets
corrugated paper
2 plastic cartons
2 plastic meat trays
Plasticine
cocktail sticks
plastic milk straws
4 plastic detergent bottles
clay and powder paint

Part 1
The corner turrets

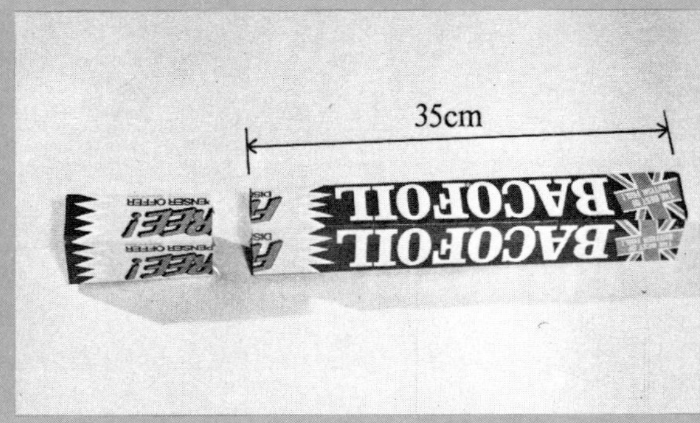

1. Take a large-size cooking foil packet. Cut it as shown. Keep the shorter length to make the southeastern corner turret (see picture 7). Take the longer section and . . .

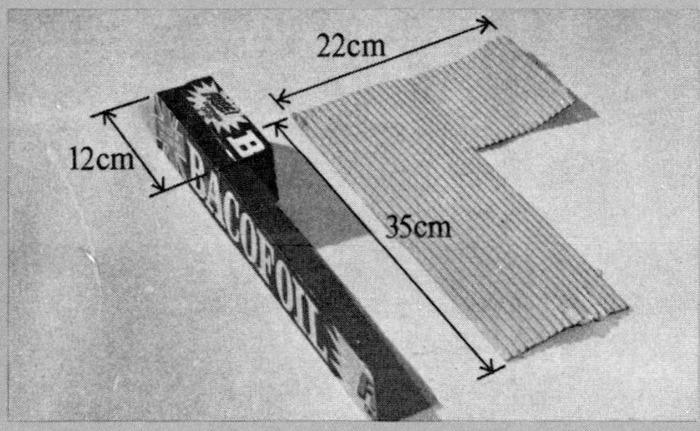

2. . . . remove two sides as shown. Cut this shape from a sheet of corrugated paper.

3. Fold the corrugated paper shape round the packet and glue it into place. This is one of the corner turrets and it fits into the southwest corner . . .

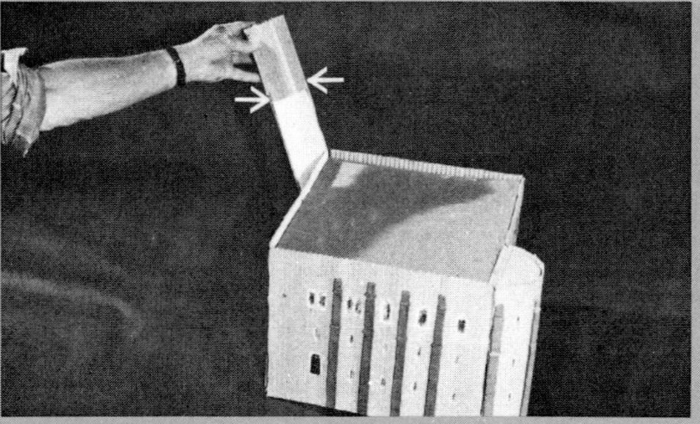

4. . . . like this. Note that slits have to be cut (arrowed) to allow the corner turret to fit into place . . .

5. . . . like this. Make a second turret for the northwest corner. Take 2 plastic cartons (the kind used for margarine or cream cheese) and cut sections out so that they will fit into the northeast corner.

6. Cut a sheet of corrugated paper and fit it round the cartons like this.

7. Fit the turret into the corner. Cut 4 Plasticine buttresses and glue them into position round the corner turret. Use the smaller section of kitchen foil packet to make the turret at the southeastern corner.

Part 2
The battlements

8. Cut strips of corrugated paper 8 cm wide and any length.

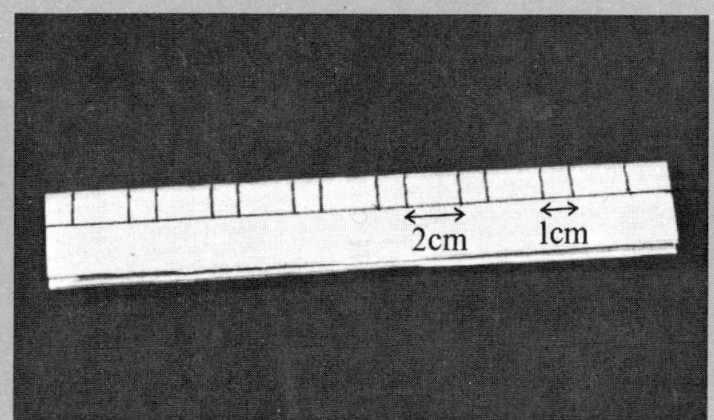

9. Fold the strips lengthways and make these marks along the folded edge.

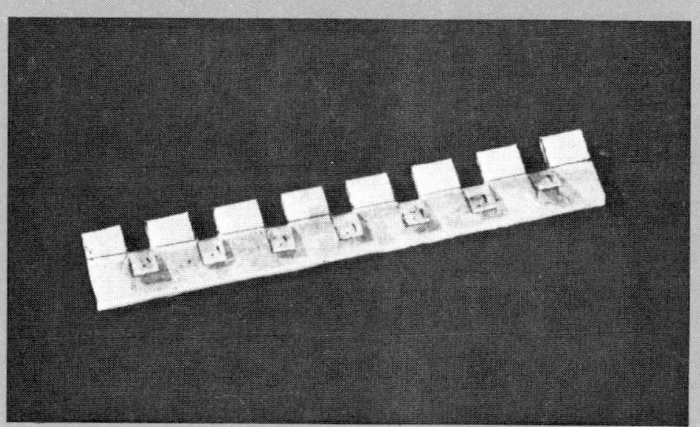

10. Cut along the lines in from the folded edge and bend the small sections back. Hold them back with glue or sticky tape.

11. Make enough to go right round the top of the Tower and glue them into position.

Part 3
The caps for the corner turrets

12. Cut the tops from 4 detergent bottles. Use Plasticine to build small square domes on top. Build them up with small pieces of Plasticine spaced round the tops as shown.

Part 4
The plinth and entrance stairs

13. Fit the domes into place. They stand on squares cut from plastic meat trays. Paint them black, if possible with glossy paint. Cocktail sticks made the spikes on top of the domes.

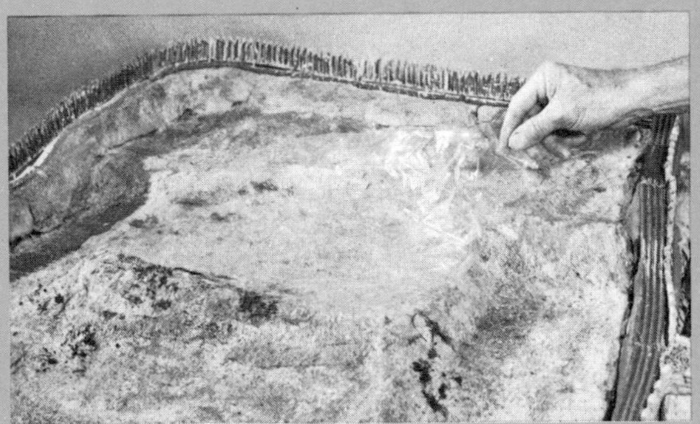

14. Cut a sheet of polythene to fit the bottom of the White Tower. Place it in position on the flat space on top of the hill in the bailey.

15. Stand the White Tower on top of the polythene. Notice that the wooden tower is still in position in the corner of the bailey. It remained there for about thirty years after the White Tower was completed in about 1099.

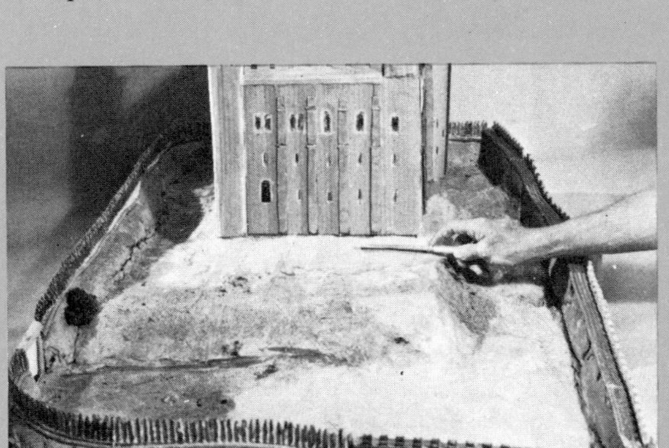

16. You can leave it there if you like or it can be removed and the space remade with wet clay. Use clay to build the plinth round the base of the White Tower . . .

17. . . . like this. Notice the rounded plinth for the apse of the chapel to stand on. Paint the plinth stone-colour and use powder paint to make grass where the wooden tower stood. (See pages 8 and 9, pictures 16 and 17.)

18. Take 12 wooden cocktail sticks. Use the point of a pair of compasses to make holes for them – 4 at the entrance to the tower and the rest to hold plastic milk straws . . .

19. . . . like this. The staircase is a strip of corrugated paper glued between 2 milk straws. Glue it into place . . .

20. . . . like this. Glue the other straws into position and cut off the surplus lengths of straw.

21. Notice the handrails on each side of the stairs. The figures are made by Airfix (their Robin Hood set) and are just the right scale.

22. This is the finished model of the White Tower as it looked when Princess Constance was kept there by Geoffrey de Mandeville. You can make it even more realistic now by making models of the stables, workshops, kitchen, bakery and living huts in the bailey. Remember that the scale is 1 cm equals 1 metre.

Note to Teachers

Each of the stories in this book is centred on an actual event or historical character. They are meant to be enjoyed as good stories, but also to be authentic, true in spirit if not in every detail.

The models are as accurate as is possible with the simple materials and methods used. Only waste materials are needed and each model has been divided into several phases of construction so that the work can be shared out among individuals or groups. You and your pupils may find alternative ways of making or finishing the models, or choose to add details imaginative or actual, especially after visiting the Tower, but it is advisable to keep to the dimensions and proportions indicated in the instructions so as to ensure that the models are properly to scale.

The 'Things to look for and to do' relate the stories and models to what pupils can see at the Tower and, in some cases, at other places.

For further information about the Tower there is the official guide *The Tower of London* and *The Young Visitors' Guide to the Tower of London*. There are also short illustrated guides to castles in general – *Castles* for England and Wales, and *Scottish Castles* – which explain the main lines of castle development and list the most interesting ones to visit. All these books are published by HMSO.

The Education Officer at the Tower provides educational services for visiting school parties and answers enquiries about the Tower. He should be contacted in the first instance by letter or telephone (01-709 0765).

Printed in England for Her Majesty's Stationery Office
by Brown Knight & Truscott Ltd, London & Tonbridge
Dd 496734 K480 7/77